A Guide to Data Science and Analytics

Navigating the Data Deluge: Tools, Techniques, and Applications

Juniper Blake

Table of Contents

INTRODUCTION

Welcome to "A Guide to Data Science and Analytics: Navigating the Data Deluge: Tools, Techniques, and Applications." In an era where data is often referred to as the new oil, understanding how to harness its power is essential for individuals and organizations. This book is your comprehensive guide through the vast and dynamic field of data science and analytics, designed to demystify the complex processes and tools used to transform raw data into actionable insights.

As you embark on this journey, you'll delve into the practical and foundational principles that underpin data science. From data collection and preprocessing to exploratory data analysis and statistical inference, we'll equip you with the essential tools and techniques data professionals use daily. You'll gain practical knowledge of languages and frameworks like Python, R, TensorFlow, and more, enhancing your professional capabilities.

The book also highlights the application of data science across various domains, including business, healthcare, social media, and government. Real-world case studies illustrate how data-driven decision-making is revolutionizing industries and improving lives. Through these examples, you'll see the tangible benefits and transformative potential of practical data analysis.

Moreover, we underscore the importance of staying updated and responsible in your data practices. As technology evolves, so do the challenges and opportunities in data science. Whether you are a beginner aiming to break into the field or a seasoned professional seeking to update your knowledge, this guide offers valuable insights and practical advice. Let's navigate the data deluge together and unlock the full potential of data science and analytics.

CHAPTER I

Welcome to the Data Age

Overview of the importance of data in the modern world

Data has become an essential component of modern life, impacting almost every area of human existence. It is impossible to overestimate the importance of data, frequently referred to as the "new oil," since it drives innovations in a wide range of fields, including government, industry, healthcare, and education. This section investigates the significance of data in the contemporary world, looking at how it might revolutionize society, how data science has developed, and what ethical issues arise when using it.

The daily generation of an unprecedented amount, velocity, and variety of data is the fundamental component of the modern data age. The amount of data generated by social media interactions, internet transactions, and sensor data from Internet of Things (IoT) devices is astounding. Big data, a term used to describe this phenomenon, presents unmatched chances for creativity and insights. Companies use this data to analyze customer behavior, streamline processes, and inform strategic choices. For example, companies such as Amazon and Netflix use data analytics to enhance consumer pleasure and loyalty by personalizing suggestions. Data has become an essential resource that gives businesses a competitive advantage in the increasingly digital economy.

The healthcare sector stands as a testament to the transformative power of data. Genomics, wearable technology, and electronic health records generate vast amounts of health-related data. Precision medicine, which tailors therapies for each patient based on genetic, environmental, and lifestyle factors, relies heavily on this wealth of information. Early disease detection, improved patient outcomes, and more efficient healthcare delivery are all made possible by data analytics. Data played a pivotal role in tracking the COVID-19 pandemic, guiding public health initiatives, and accelerating vaccine development. Thus, the global health landscape is significantly shaped by the ability to gather, analyze, and interpret health data, instilling a sense of hope and optimism for the future of medicine.

Another area where data has a significant impact is education. Understanding student performance and engagement is changing due to learning analytics, which analyzes educational data to improve learning outcomes. Using data, educators can improve teaching tactics, identify at-risk kids, and tailor learning experiences. Data is used by Massive Open Online Courses (MOOCs) and other e-learning platforms to monitor student progress, improve course material, and offer immediate feedback. By filling in gaps in conventional learning environments, this data-driven strategy improves the educational experience and democratizes access to high-quality education.

Data-driven insights also greatly help public policy and government. Data analytics makes effective resource allocation, crime prevention, and catastrophe management possible. Predictive policing, for instance, makes better use of resource allocation by using data to pinpoint probable crime hotspots. Data is used in urban planning to create "smart cities," which enhance public services, transportation, and infrastructure through technology and data analytics. Furthermore, open data projects and data transparency improve citizen participation and government accountability, promoting an informed and engaged society.

The emergence of the data age raises serious ethical and privacy issues, notwithstanding its many advantages. Large-scale personal data collecting, archiving, and analysis raises concerns about security, abuse potential, and permission. Scandals and high-profile data breaches, like the one involving Cambridge Analytica, highlight the dangers of data abuse. Establishing robust ethical frameworks and regulatory laws is crucial to safeguarding individuals' rights and ensuring responsible data use as data becomes increasingly incorporated into our daily lives. It involves putting data privacy rules into effect, such as the General Data Protection Regulation (GDPR) in the European Union, which establishes strict guidelines for privacy and data protection.

Navigating the intricacies of the data age has been made more accessible by the discipline's progress. And extract valuable insights from data, data science brings together domain expertise, computer science, and statistics. The possibilities of data science have been significantly enhanced by the development of sophisticated machine learning algorithms and artificial intelligence (AI). With these tools, analyzing massive, complicated datasets and finding previously undiscovered patterns and trends is now possible. Machine learning transforms domains like natural language processing, predictive analytics, and picture and speech recognition. These technologies improve efficiency and allow for more precise and intelligent decision-making by automating analytical activities.

Additionally, data visualization is essential to making data comprehensible and accessible. Tools like Tableau, Power BI, and D3.js make data-driven storytelling easier by turning unstructured data into understandable visual representations. When there is effective data visualization, stakeholders are better able to understand complex information, recognize important insights, and make decisions. For instance, dashboards and interactive reports in business give executives immediate access to performance metrics and enable them to act quickly in response to shifting market conditions.

The future will be shaped by how data is integrated with emerging technology as we progress in the digital age. More data will be generated by the spread of IoT devices, improving our capacity to monitor and optimize different systems continuously. Blockchain technology offers decentralized, tamper-proof data storage options, which promise to answer data security and integrity issues. Furthermore, the intersection of data science with disciplines like environmental science and biotechnology presents an opportunity to tackle some of the most critical problems facing the globe today, from fighting climate change to finding cures for diseases.

Data has a significant and diverse role in the modern world. It stimulates creativity, provides insight for decision-making, and improves productivity in several industries. But the power of data also demands that its application be done with caution and morality. It is essential to strike a balance between the obligations that come with data and the opportunities it presents as we manage the tsunami of data. By promoting a culture that values ethical data practices and the utilization of data science and analytics breakthroughs, we can fully utilize data to build a more knowledgeable, effective, and fair society.

The rise of big data and its implications

The rise of big data represents one of the most transformative developments in the digital age, fundamentally altering how individuals, businesses, and governments operate. Big data refers to the vast volumes of structured and unstructured data generated at unprecedented speed from various sources, including social media, sensors, transaction records, and more. This surge in data availability has profound implications, influencing decision-making processes, driving innovation, and presenting new challenges and opportunities across various sectors.

The proliferation of internet-connected devices, social media platforms, and advanced data collection technologies primarily drives big data's exponential growth. For instance, the Internet of Things (IoT) connects everyday devices like smartphones, wearables, and household appliances, continuously generating data about users' behaviors, preferences, and interactions. Similarly, social media platforms capture vast amounts of user-generated content, ranging from text and images to videos and geolocation data. This constant flow of information contributes to the immense data reservoirs that characterize the extensive data landscape.

One of the most significant implications of big data is its ability to enhance decision-making. Organizations leverage big data analytics to gain deeper insights into their operations, customers, and markets. By analyzing large datasets, businesses can identify patterns and trends that were previously undetectable, allowing for more informed and strategic decisions. For example, retailers use big data to optimize inventory management, personalize marketing efforts, and improve customer service. Financial institutions analyze transaction data to detect fraudulent activities, assess credit risk, and develop new financial products. Big data analytics enables precision medicine, predictive diagnostics, and improved patient care by integrating data from electronic health records, medical imaging, and genomics.

Moreover, big data drives innovation by providing the raw material for new technologies and business models. Machine learning and artificial intelligence (AI) algorithms, which rely heavily on large datasets, have made significant advancements thanks to big data. These technologies can analyze vast amounts of information quickly and accurately, leading to innovations in fields such as autonomous vehicles, natural language processing, and personalized recommendations. Companies like Google, Amazon, and Netflix use big data to refine their AI models, enhancing their products and services and delivering personalized experiences to users.

The rise of big data also impacts public policy and governance. Governments and public agencies utilize big data to improve service delivery, enhance public safety, and make data-driven policy decisions. For instance, predictive analytics can help law enforcement agencies allocate resources more effectively, while urban planners use data from sensors and social media to monitor and manage city infrastructure. During the COVID-19 pandemic, big data played a crucial role in tracking the spread of the virus, informing public health responses, and accelerating vaccine development. These applications highlight how big data can contribute to more efficient and responsive governance.

However, the rise of big data also presents significant challenges, particularly regarding privacy and security. The massive scale of data collection raises concerns about the extent to which individuals' personal information is being monitored and analyzed. High-profile data breaches and misuse of personal data, such as the Cambridge Analytica scandal, have underscored the risks associated with big data. These incidents have increased scrutiny and calls for stricter data protection regulations. Legislation like the General Data Protection Regulation (GDPR) in the European Union aims to safeguard personal data by imposing stringent requirements on how organizations collect, store, and process information.

In addition to privacy concerns, the sheer volume and complexity of big data pose technical challenges. Traditional data processing tools and techniques often need to be improved for handling big data, necessitating the development of new technologies and infrastructures. Distributed computing frameworks like Hadoop and Spark have emerged to address these challenges, enabling the storage and processing of large datasets across multiple servers. Cloud computing platforms provide scalable and cost-effective solutions for big data analytics, allowing organizations to access vast computational resources on demand.

Ethical considerations are another critical aspect of big data's rise. The potential for biased algorithms and discriminatory practices is a significant concern, as machine learning models trained on biased data can perpetuate and amplify existing inequalities. Ensuring fairness, accountability, and transparency in big data analytics is essential to mitigate these risks. Organizations must adopt ethical guidelines and best practices for data collection and analysis, including diverse data sourcing, rigorous testing, and continuous monitoring of algorithmic performance.

In conclusion, the rise of big data marks a paradigm shift in how we generate, analyze, and utilize information. Its implications are far-reaching, transforming decision-making, driving innovation, and reshaping public policy and governance. While big data offers tremendous opportunities, it also presents significant challenges concerning privacy, security, and ethics. As we navigate the complexities of the substantial data era, it is crucial to balance the benefits of data-driven insights with the need to protect individual rights and ensure ethical practices. By doing so, we can harness the full potential of big data to create a more informed, efficient, and equitable world.

Objectives and structure of the book

A thorough resource for newcomers and seasoned pros in data science and analytics, "A Guide to Data Science and Analytics: Navigating the Data Deluge: Tools, Techniques, and Applications" is painstakingly crafted. This book's primary goal is to demystify the intricate procedures involved in data science by providing readers with a systematic and valuable framework for comprehending and utilizing data-driven approaches. Through an in-depth examination of fundamental ideas, cutting-edge techniques, and practical applications, the book seeks to provide readers with the information and abilities they need to succeed in this quickly developing field.

The book is divided into four sections, each focusing on a crucial area of analytics and data science. By starting with the fundamentals and working their way up to more complicated subjects, this modular method guarantees that readers may gradually increase their comprehension. The introductory section, "Foundations of Data Science and Analytics," establishes the background by outlining the core ideas of data science. The definition, application, and historical development of data science are explored in this part, along with the duties and responsibilities of several types of data professionals, including data scientists, data analysts, and data engineers. This section guarantees readers understand the key terms and topics in more detail in the following chapters by providing a solid foundation.

The first section builds on the core knowledge by outlining the data science process and stressing the significance of each stage, from data collection to analysis and interpretation. It covers the typical difficulties at these points and presents the frameworks and technologies that make the data science workflow easier. The section also discusses the many forms of data, their origins, and the moral issues related to data security and privacy. This all-encompassing introduction sets readers up for subsequent in-depth conversations by giving a thorough rundown.

The second section, "Tools and Techniques," delves further into data science applications. This part is essential for readers who wish to become familiar with the instruments and procedures used in the field on a practical level. Starting with data collecting and preparation procedures, it provides an understanding of different data collection, cleaning, and format conversion approaches. This section emphasizes the need for clean and well-structured data before any meaningful analysis can occur by concentrating on the preliminary stages of data analysis.

The following section moves on to exploratory data analysis (EDA), where readers will discover how to use summary statistics and visualization to find patterns and insights. EDA is a vital first step in deciphering the data's underlying structure, guiding further modeling and analysis. After that, the topic shifts to statistical analysis and inference, giving readers the statistical foundation they need to test hypotheses, create regression models, and derive reliable conclusions from data.

This section includes a lot of material on machine learning, with chapters covering fundamental and sophisticated methods. Along with essential algorithms like neural networks, clustering, regression, and classification, readers are exposed to supervised, unsupervised, and reinforcement learning, among other forms of machine learning. The book also covers advanced subjects, including time series analysis, deep learning, and natural language processing (NLP), which provides readers with a thorough grasp of the most recent advancements in data science techniques. There is a focus on practical implementation, with exercises and examples made possible by well-known programs like Python, R, TensorFlow, and PyTorch.

The final section, "Applications of Data Science and Analytics," provides examples of how data science is applied in many industries. This section aims to demonstrate how real-world problems can be solved using the theoretical understanding and practical abilities acquired in the earlier sections. Case studies and examples from various Industries, including business, healthcare, social media, and government, illustrate data science's adaptability and transformational potential. The benefits of data-driven decision-making for corporate operations, healthcare results, marketing strategies, and public policy will be demonstrated to readers. The book closes the knowledge gap between theory and practice by examining various applications and explaining the real-world advantages of data science.

The last section, "Future Trends and Ethical Considerations," discusses how data science is developing. Emerging topics like advances in big data technologies, artificial intelligence, and the future of data visualization are covered in this section. It also addresses the moral dilemmas data science raises, such as bias, equity, openness, and data privacy. The book equips readers to responsibly and ethically navigate the future of data science by emphasizing these crucial subjects.

Finally, "A Guide to Data Science and Analytics: Navigating the Data Deluge: Tools, Techniques, and Applications" is organized to offer a thorough, realistic, and morally conscious overview of the data science discipline. From basic ideas to sophisticated techniques and practical applications, the book gives readers the information and abilities they need to succeed in the data-driven world. Irrespective of your experience level, this guide provides insightful analysis and valuable recommendations to help you leverage data science to the fullest extent possible in your career.

CHAPTER II

Understanding Data Science

Definition and scope of data science

The multidisciplinary subject of data science uses scientific procedures, systems, algorithms, and methodologies to glean insights and knowledge from structured and unstructured data. Its rise has been fueled by the exponential increase in data produced by digital activities and processing and storage power improvements. Data science is essential in today's data-driven society because of its broad definition and range of disciplines, methods, and applications.

Data science is fundamentally about taking actionable insights from data. The first step in this process is data collection, which involves gathering raw data from various sources, including sensors, databases, social media platforms, and transactional systems. The following phase is data cleaning and preprocessing, which includes addressing missing values, resolving discrepancies, and formatting the data appropriately for analysis. These preliminary actions are crucial because they guarantee the authenticity and dependability of the data, which directly affects the quality of the conclusions drawn from it.

Exploratory data analysis (EDA) is performed after data preprocessing to uncover underlying patterns, distributions, and correlations in the data. EDA summarizes the key features of the data using statistical methods and data visualization software. This stage is essential because it produces hypotheses for additional research, helps identify significant factors, and detects anomalies. R and Python (with libraries like Pandas, Matplotlib, and Seaborn) are frequently used for this.

The analytical part of data science includes a variety of techniques, from sophisticated machine learning algorithms to conventional statistical analysis. Regression analysis, inferential statistics, and hypothesis testing are some methods used in statistical analysis that aid in inferring patterns and conclusions from data. A kind of artificial intelligence called machine learning uses data to train algorithms to categorize information or make predictions without needing to be specifically designed for every task. Supervised learning (e.g., decision trees, linear regression), unsupervised learning (e.g., principal component analysis, clustering), and reinforcement learning are essential machine learning approaches.

One of data science's distinguishing characteristics is its multidisciplinary nature. It integrates domain-specific knowledge with experience in computer science, statistics, and mathematics to address complicated issues. For example, in addition to their technical skills, a data scientist in the healthcare industry must be familiar with clinical protocols and medical terminology. Thanks to this interdisciplinary approach, data scientists may adapt their techniques to unavoidable circumstances, guaranteeing their findings are applicable and valuable.

Data science is far more than just data analysis. Models and algorithms must be implemented into production systems to produce real-time insights and facilitate decision-making. MLOps (machine learning operations) or data engineering are standard terms for this branch of data science. It involves activities including model deployment, monitoring, and maintenance to ensure that analytical models function correctly over time and can adjust to new data.

Data science is also essential for creating data-driven goods and services. Businesses like Google, Netflix, and Amazon have based their business strategies on data science. Using data science, Amazon makes product recommendations to users based on their past browsing and purchasing activity. By using it to tailor content recommendations, Netflix increases user pleasure and engagement. Google uses data science in numerous areas, including ad targeting and search engines. These examples show how data science can spur innovation and provide significant advantages over competitors.

Data science significantly impacts public policy and social welfare, in addition to the business sector. Governments and nonprofits use data science to address social issues like environmental sustainability, healthcare, and education. Predictive analytics, for instance, can be used to identify at-risk students in school systems, allocate healthcare resources more effectively, and model the effects of climate change to influence policy decisions. These case studies highlight how data science may advance societal welfare.

Data science has a lot of promise but has certain drawbacks. Security and privacy of data is one of the main issues. Sensitive personal data is frequently collected and analyzed in enormous amounts, which raises questions regarding how this data is shared, processed, and preserved. Critical challenges that data scientists must face are ethical considerations, such as bias in algorithms and transparency in decision-making processes. Retaining public confidence and using data responsibly requires that data science activities adhere to ethical standards and legal requirements.

Moreover, the swift advancement in data science demands ongoing education and adjustment: new tools, methods, and best practices are rapidly being developed in the area. To continue being productive in their positions, data scientists need to keep up with the most recent developments and be open to picking up new abilities. Data science is a dynamic area that demands a commitment to lifelong learning and is both exciting and challenging.

To sum up, data science is a broad field that blends several academic specialties to glean valuable insights from data. Its scope spans various approaches, from statistical analysis to machine learning, and encompasses data gathering, preparation, analysis, and deployment. Data science's interdisciplinary nature makes it applicable to various fields, fostering innovation and tackling complex problems. Although it brings many ethical and technical concerns that must be carefully managed, it also offers enormous opportunities. The number and significance of data will only increase, and data science will play an increasingly important role in determining how enterprises and society develop in the future.

History and evolution of data science

Data science's origins and progress can be linked to the early advances in information theory, computer science, and statistics. Although the name "data science" is relatively new, having emerged in the early 21st century, the underlying ideas and techniques have existed for much longer. Data science has roots in fields like mathematics, which gave statistical analysis and probability theory their theoretical foundations. Scientists like Francis Galton and Karl Pearson, who conducted ground-breaking research in regression analysis, correlation, and hypothesis testing in the late 19th and early 20th centuries, set the foundation for contemporary statistical techniques.

The emergence of computers in the mid-20th century marked a significant milestone in the evolution of data science. The advent of electronic computers enabled the processing and analysis of large datasets, paving the way for the development of computational statistics and data analysis techniques. In the 1950s and 1960s, researchers such as John Tukey and John W. Tukey pioneered exploratory data analysis (EDA), introducing graphical methods and statistical tools to uncover patterns and trends in data. These early efforts laid the foundation for modern data visualization techniques, crucial in data science today.

Another critical development in the history of data science is the rise of machine learning and artificial intelligence (AI). The roots of machine learning can be traced back to the 1940s and 1950s when researchers like Alan Turing and Marvin Minsky laid the theoretical groundwork for intelligent machines. The invention of the perceptron by Frank Rosenblatt in 1957 marked a significant milestone in the development of artificial neural networks, an essential subfield of machine learning. However, progress in machine learning could have been faster due to limitations in computational power and the lack of large-scale datasets.

The turning point for machine learning came in the late 20th century with the advent of the internet and the proliferation of digital technologies. The availability of vast amounts of digital data, coupled with advancements in computational resources and algorithms, revolutionized the field of machine learning. Researchers developed new techniques, such as support vector machines, decision trees, and random forests, which enabled more accurate and scalable data analysis. The development of deep learning algorithms, particularly convolutional neural networks (CNNs) and recurrent neural networks (RNNs), further propelled the field of machine learning, leading to breakthroughs in areas such as computer vision, natural language processing, and speech recognition.

The term "data science" gained prominence in the early 21st century as organizations increasingly recognized the importance of extracting insights from data to gain a competitive advantage. In 2001, William S. Cleveland introduced the concept of data science as an interdisciplinary field that combines statistics, computer science, and domain expertise to analyze and interpret complex datasets. The explosion of big data in the following years further fueled the demand for data science skills, leading to the emergence of specialized educational programs, certifications, and job roles.

Data science has become ubiquitous today, with applications across diverse industries and domains. Companies and organizations rely on data scientists to extract actionable insights from data, inform decision-making processes, and drive innovation. Data science techniques are used in finance, healthcare, marketing, cybersecurity, and beyond, shaping how businesses operate and society functions.

Future developments in technology and methodology are anticipated to propel the field's advancement further. The emergence of data-driven technologies, such as advanced computing, quantum computing, and blockchain, can completely transform the industry by opening up new avenues for data analysis research and development. Ethical considerations, including data privacy, bias in algorithms, and transparency in decision-making, will also play an increasingly important role in shaping the future of data science. As data science continues to evolve, its impact on industries, economies, and societies worldwide is poised to grow, making it one of the most dynamic and influential fields of the 21st century.

Key roles in data science: Data Scientist, Data Analyst, Data Engineer

In today's data-driven world, data science has become a vital field encompassing various roles that help extract value and insights from data. Data scientists, data analysts, and data engineers are some of the most essential positions in data science. In the data ecosystem, each of these professions contributes to the gathering, processing, analyzing, and interpreting of data in a unique but interrelated way.

A data scientist's position is frequently seen as the focal point of data science. The main task of data scientists is to create and apply sophisticated analytical models that can find patterns in massive information and forecast future events. They are highly knowledgeable about programming, machine learning, and statistics. They organize and clean data, run complex algorithms, and then evaluate the output to guide company strategy. When creating machine learning models, data scientists usually employ tools like TensorFlow or PyTorch and computer languages like Python or R. Their observations support businesses in making data-driven decisions that involve forecasting consumer behavior, streamlining processes, or spotting untapped market niches. Owing to their diverse skill set, data scientists are frequently called the "unicorns" of the data industry. They successfully communicate their findings by fusing strong analytical skills with business acumen and good communication.

Conversely, data analysts emphasize using data analysis and exploration to produce insights that can be set to use. Their main objective is to analyze data collection to find trends, patterns, and anomalies that help guide business decisions. When presenting their findings in an understandable format, data analysts usually utilize tools like Tableau or Power BI for data visualization, SQL for database querying, and Excel for data manipulation. Data analysts are vital to making data accessible and valuable for stakeholders who are not technical, even though they might not be as involved in advanced modeling and machine learning techniques as Data Scientists are. They are skilled in creating dashboards, reports, and visualizations that help monitor the success of company goals and highlight key performance indicators (KPIs). By using actual data, their work guarantees that decision-makers have a precise and accurate understanding of the corporate environment.

A data engineer's work is primarily concerned with the architecture and infrastructure of data systems. Data engineers design, construct, and maintain the systems and pipelines that enable effective data collection, storage, and access. They are skilled in languages like SQL, Python, and Java and work with massive databases. Their proficiency with cloud platforms like AWS and Azure and big data technologies like Spark and Hadoop allows them to handle enormous volumes of data and guarantee that Data Scientists and Data Analysts can access it for analysis. Data engineers create and enhance data pipelines to ensure the accuracy and efficiency of the data. They are essential to the data lifecycle because they ensure the data is processed appropriately and quickly from its unprocessed condition to one that allows for analysis and decision-making.

Data Scientists, Data Analysts, and Data Engineers collaborate and overlap significantly while having separate focus areas. To guarantee that the data needed for analysis is easily accessible and clean, a Data Scientist and a Data Engineer may collaborate closely. Similarly, data engineers build and maintain the databases and pipelines that supply the data required by data analysts for their reports and visualizations. This dependency emphasizes how crucial a business must have a unified data strategy, where one job supports and enhances the others to accomplish shared objectives.

To summarize, each of the three primary professions in data science—data scientist, data analyst, and data engineer—brings special abilities and duties critical to the data ecosystem. Data engineers create and manage the infrastructure that supports data processing and storage, data scientists generate sophisticated analytical modeling and insights, and data analysts convert data into valuable business knowledge. These positions allow businesses to use data to improve operations, make well-informed decisions, and obtain a competitive advantage in the market. The cooperation and synergy between these jobs will be essential to realizing data science's full potential as data's significance grows.

CHAPTER III

The Data Science Process

Steps in the data science lifecycle: data collection, cleaning, analysis, and interpretation

The entire process of turning unprocessed data into insightful knowledge and valuable intelligence is known as data science. Data gathering, cleaning, analysis, and interpretation are some of the crucial elements in this process, referred to as the "data science lifecycle." Every stage is essential to guarantee the relevance, quality, and dependability of the insights produced and empower enterprises to make data-driven decisions.

The first step in the data science lifecycle is data collection. It involves gathering raw data from various sources, including databases, web scraping, sensors, social media, etc. The quality and quantity of data collected are crucial, as they lay the foundation for all subsequent steps. Effective data collection requires a clear understanding of the problem to be solved and the type of data needed to address it. For example, a company looking to analyze customer behavior might collect data from purchase histories, website interactions, and customer feedback. Data scientists must also consider ethical and legal implications during this stage, ensuring that data is collected with proper consent and in compliance with privacy regulations.

Once the data is collected, the next step is data cleaning, also known as data preprocessing. Raw data is often messy and incomplete, containing errors, duplicates, and inconsistencies that can skew analysis results. Data cleaning involves identifying and rectifying these issues to improve data quality. This process includes handling missing values, correcting inaccuracies, standardizing formats, and removing duplicates. For instance, missing values can be addressed by imputation, where missing data points are filled in based on statistical methods or domain knowledge. Outliers, which can significantly affect the analysis, are corrected or removed if deemed erroneous. Data cleaning is a meticulous and time-consuming process but is essential for ensuring the reliability of the analysis.

After the data has been cleaned, the next phase is data analysis. This step involves exploring the cleaned data to uncover patterns, correlations, and trends. Data analysis can be divided into exploratory data analysis (EDA) and confirmatory data analysis (CDA). EDA is an initial investigation where data scientists use statistical methods and visualization tools to understand the data's underlying structure and generate hypotheses. Tools such as histograms, scatter plots, and box plots help visualize distributions and relationships within the data. CDA, on the other hand, involves testing these hypotheses using more rigorous statistical techniques and models. During this stage, data scientists might apply machine learning algorithms to build predictive models or identify clusters and segments within the data. Data analysis aims to extract meaningful insights that can inform decision-making and strategy.

The final step in the data science lifecycle is data interpretation, which involves translating the results of the data analysis into actionable insights that non-technical stakeholders can understand and utilize. Practical data interpretation requires clear communication and visualization skills. Data scientists must present their findings in a way that highlights key insights and supports decision-making processes. That often involves creating dashboards, reports, and visualizations that convey complex information in a digestible format. For example, a data scientist might use a combination of charts, graphs, and narrative explanations to show how customer behavior trends can impact marketing strategies. Additionally, interpretation includes assessing the limitations and assumptions of the analysis to provide a balanced perspective. This step is crucial for ensuring that the insights generated are accurate, practical, and relevant to the business context.

Throughout the entire data science lifecycle, an iterative approach is often employed. Insights gained during analysis and interpretation can lead to new questions and hypotheses, prompting further data collection and refinement. This cyclical nature of the process ensures continuous improvement and deeper understanding over time.

In conclusion, the data science process, encompassing data collection, cleaning, analysis, and interpretation, is a systematic approach to transforming raw data into valuable insights. Each step is critical, requiring specific skills and tools to ensure the results' accuracy, reliability, and relevance. By following this lifecycle, organizations can harness the power of data to drive informed decision-making, optimize operations, and gain a competitive advantage. The iterative and interconnected nature of these steps highlights data science's dynamic and evolving nature, emphasizing the importance of a robust and flexible approach to handling data.

Importance of each step and common challenges

The data science process—which includes data collection, cleaning, analysis, and interpretation—is essential to turning raw data into insightful knowledge. Every stage in this process is vital, with its difficulties and significance. Knowing these can make navigating the data science difficulties easier and guarantee reliable, valuable results.

Data collection is the data science lifecycle's first and most crucial stage. It entails obtaining unprocessed data from various sources, including web scraping, databases, APIs, sensors, and more. The fundamental function of data collecting is what makes it so important; the extent and caliber of the data gathered directly affect the actions that follow. While incomplete or poor-quality data can result in conclusions that need to be corrected, complete and high-quality data allows for accurate analysis and trustworthy insights. Data collection has its challenges, though. Relevant data accessibility is a typical problem that proprietary restrictions or privacy concerns might hamper.

Additionally, data can be fragmented across multiple sources, requiring significant integration effort. Ensuring ethical standards and compliance with data privacy laws, such as GDPR, further complicates the process. Overcoming these challenges requires a strategic approach involving careful planning and using advanced tools and technologies to streamline data collection and ensure its integrity.

Following data collection, the next step is data cleaning or preprocessing. This step is essential because raw data is often messy, containing errors, duplicates, and inconsistencies that can skew analysis results. Data cleaning ensures the data is accurate, complete, and formatted correctly. The importance of this step cannot be overstated, as the famous adage "garbage in, garbage out" highlights the direct correlation between data quality and the reliability of analysis. However, data cleaning presents several challenges. Identifying and correcting errors can be time-consuming, and deciding how to handle missing or inconsistent data often involves subjective judgment calls that can introduce bias. Automating data-cleaning processes can help, but it requires sophisticated algorithms and domain knowledge to address these issues effectively. Balancing thoroughness with efficiency is another challenge, as overly meticulous cleaning can delay the entire data science project.

Once the data is cleaned, the analysis phase begins. This step involves exploring the data to uncover patterns, trends, and relationships. Data analysis is crucial for generating insights that can inform decision-making and strategy. It includes exploratory data analysis (EDA) to understand the data's structure and confirmatory data analysis (CDA) to test hypotheses and build predictive models. The significance of data analysis lies in its ability to transform raw data into actionable intelligence, providing a basis for strategic decisions. However, this step is also challenging. One common difficulty is selecting the appropriate analytical methods and tools, as different techniques can yield varying results. Additionally, the complexity of statistical and machine learning models can be daunting, requiring a deep understanding of both the methodologies and the specific application domain. Ensuring the reproducibility and robustness of results is another challenge, necessitating careful validation and testing of models.

The final step in the data science lifecycle is data interpretation, which involves translating analytical findings into actionable insights. This step is vital for making data understandable and useful for non-technical stakeholders. Practical data interpretation requires clear communication and visualization skills to present complex information quickly. The importance of this step lies in its impact on decision-making; well-interpreted data can drive strategic initiatives and operational improvements. However, interpreting data poses its own set of challenges. One major issue is avoiding misinterpretation or overgeneralization of results, which can lead to incorrect conclusions and decisions. Communicating uncertainty and limitations is essential but often challenging. Additionally, creating compelling and accurate visualizations requires technical skills and an understanding of the audience's needs and perspectives.

In conclusion, each step of the data science process—data collection, cleaning, analysis, and interpretation—plays a crucial role in transforming raw data into valuable insights. While each step is essential, they are also interdependent; the success of one phase often hinges on the effectiveness of the previous ones. Each step presents unique challenges, from data accessibility and quality issues in collection and cleaning to methodological complexities in analysis and communication barriers in interpretation. Addressing these challenges requires technical expertise, strategic planning, and effective communication. By understanding the importance and intricacies of each step, data scientists can navigate the complexities of the data science process and generate reliable, actionable insights that drive informed decision-making and strategic success.

Tools and frameworks supporting the data science process

The field of data science has seen remarkable growth in recent years, driven by the exponential increase in data availability and advancements in computational power. The tools and frameworks that support the data science process are central to this growth, enabling data scientists to collect, clean, analyze, and interpret data efficiently. These tools and frameworks are designed to handle the complexities of large datasets, provide sophisticated analytical capabilities, and facilitate clear communication of results. They span various stages of the data science lifecycle and are crucial for transforming raw data into actionable insights.

Tools and frameworks are essential for efficiently gathering data from diverse sources in the data collection phase. SQL (Structured Query Language) is a fundamental tool for retrieving data from relational databases. It allows data scientists to write queries that extract specific data subsets from vast databases. For unstructured data, web scraping tools like BeautifulSoup and Scrapy are widely used to collect data from websites. These tools can navigate through web pages, extract relevant information, and save it in a structured format for further analysis. Additionally, APIs (Application Programming Interfaces) provide a streamlined way to access data from various services and platforms, such as social media or financial databases. Tools like Postman and Insomnia facilitate the testing and integration of these APIs, ensuring that data collection processes are robust and efficient.

Once the data is collected, it needs to be cleaned and preprocessed, a step critical for ensuring the accuracy and reliability of the analysis. Python, with libraries like Pandas and NumPy, is a dominant tool in this phase. Pandas provide robust data structures for manipulating and analyzing data, making it easier to handle missing values, remove duplicates, and convert data types. On the other hand, NumPy offers support for large, multi-dimensional arrays and matrices, along with a collection of mathematical functions to operate on these arrays. For more complex data-cleaning tasks, frameworks like Apache Spark are invaluable. Spark's distributed computing capabilities allow it to process large datasets across multiple nodes, making it possible to clean and preprocess data at scale. Its DataFrame API, similar to Pandas, provides an easy-to-use data manipulation and transformation interface.

Data analysis, the core of the data science process, is supported by various tools and frameworks that offer advanced analytical and machine-learning capabilities. Python remains a leading language for data analysis, with libraries such as SciPy and Scikit-Learn providing comprehensive support for statistical analysis and machine learning algorithms. SciPy builds on NumPy to offer additional modules for optimization, integration, interpolation, eigenvalue problems, and other advanced computations. Scikit-Learn simplifies the implementation of machine learning algorithms, offering tools for model selection, evaluation, and validation. For deep learning, frameworks like TensorFlow and PyTorch are prominent. TensorFlow, developed by Google, is an open-source platform for machine learning that provides a comprehensive ecosystem for building and deploying machine learning models. PyTorch, created by Facebook's AI Research lab, is known for its flexibility and ease of use, particularly in research and development settings. Both frameworks support GPU acceleration, enabling the efficient training of large-scale neural networks.

Visualization is a crucial aspect of data analysis, and tools like Matplotlib, Seaborn, and Tableau play a significant role in this phase. Matplotlib is a versatile plotting library for Python that allows data scientists to create static, animated, and interactive visualizations. Seaborn, built on Matplotlib, provides a high-level interface for drawing attractive and informative statistical graphics. For more interactive and shareable visualizations, Tableau is a powerful tool. It allows users to create dashboards and reports that can be easily shared with stakeholders, making complex data insights accessible to non-technical audiences.

The final step in the data science process, data interpretation, often involves presenting findings that are understandable and actionable for decision-makers. Tools like Jupyter Notebooks are invaluable in this phase. Jupyter Notebooks provide an interactive computing environment where data scientists can combine code, visualizations, and narrative text. This makes it easy to document the data analysis process, share insights, and collaborate with others. Communication tools like

Microsoft PowerPoint and Google Slides are often used to create presentations summarizing key findings and recommendations. Integrating data visualizations and interactive elements from tools like Tableau can enhance these presentations, making them more engaging and impactful.

Cloud-based platforms have become increasingly important in supporting the entire data science process in recent years. Platforms like Google Cloud Platform (GCP), Amazon Web Services (AWS), and Microsoft Azure offer services that facilitate data collection, storage, processing, and analysis. These platforms provide scalable infrastructure and managed services for big data processing (e.g., Google BigQuery, AWS Redshift), machine learning (e.g., Google AI Platform, AWS SageMaker), and data storage (e.g., Google Cloud Storage, AWS S3). Integrating these services within a unified platform streamlines the data science workflow, allowing data scientists to focus more on analysis and less on infrastructure management.

In conclusion, the tools and frameworks supporting the data science process are indispensable for efficiently transforming raw data into actionable insights. They facilitate each stage of the data science lifecycle—from data collection and cleaning to analysis and interpretation—ensuring that data scientists can handle the complexities of modern datasets. By leveraging these tools and frameworks, organizations can unlock the full potential of their data, driving informed decision-making and strategic growth. As the field of data science continues to evolve, the development and adoption of more advanced and integrated tools will further enhance the capabilities and impact of data-driven insights.

CHAPTER IV

Data Types and Sources

Structured vs. unstructured data

Understanding the many kinds of data and where they come from is essential in data science to glean insightful information and make wise judgments. Unstructured and structured data are the two primary categories into which data may be divided. Every kind has different traits, advantages, and difficulties, and they come from various places. Designing successful data strategies and realizing the potential of data requires understanding the distinctions between these different forms of data and the sources that supply them.

Information arranged in a set format, usually found in spreadsheets or relational databases, is called structured data. Because of its predetermined schema and consistent format, this kind of data is well-organized and easy to find. Typically, structured data is kept in tables with rows and columns, where each row denotes a record, and each column represents a specific attribute. Product inventory, customer information, and financial transactions are a few examples of structured data. Customer relationship management (CRM), enterprise resource planning (ERP), and transactional systems are familiar sources of this data. Structured data can be evaluated using typical data processing methods and query languages like SQL because of its organized form. The main benefit of structured data is that it's simple to use, with a uniform format that makes analysis, retrieval, and storage quick and easy.

On the other hand, unstructured data needs to fit into rows and columns neatly or have a predetermined structure. This data is much more sophisticated and diversified since it contains text, photos, audio, video, and more. Emails, movies, audio recordings, social network posts, and sensor data are familiar unstructured data sources. Unstructured data, unlike structured data, is usually stored in its original format and necessitates specific processing and analysis methods and tools. For example, natural language processing (NLP) and text mining are used to examine textual data, whereas computer vision techniques are used for picture and video analysis. Unstructured data is complex to work with because of its complexity and unpredictability. More processing power and sophisticated analytical methods are needed to extract insights from unstructured data. However, compared to structured data, the richness of unstructured data frequently offers better insights and a more thorough understanding of events.

The data sources are also included in classifying structured and unstructured data. System-generated and well-defined are common characteristics of structured data sources. These consist of transactional systems that generate repeatable and consistent records, relational databases, and data warehouses. One source of structured data is the sales database of a retail business, which keeps tabs on employee performance, inventory levels, and consumer purchases. Because these systems guarantee data consistency and integrity, they are dependable resources for reporting and analysis. Structured data sources depend on regulatory compliance, performance monitoring, and operational reporting.

Unstructured data sources, however, come in various forms and are frequently created by users. They include various digital information produced and disseminated on multiple platforms. Social networking sites like Facebook, Instagram, and Twitter produce large volumes of unstructured data from posts, comments, and multimedia content. Email servers also hold unstructured data in the form of attachments and messages. Besides this, unstructured data sources consist of multimedia information from digital libraries, consumer reviews, and documents kept in enterprise content management systems. The spread of Internet of Things (IoT) devices has increased the number of unstructured data sources by gathering data in real-time from sensors integrated into various settings, including smart homes, industrial machinery, and medical devices.

Unstructured data presents some difficulties, yet its analysis can have significant advantages. For instance, sentiment analysis of social media posts can offer up-to-date information on consumer satisfaction and public opinion. Businesses may enhance their goods and services by examining consumer comments and evaluations. Unstructured data from research articles, clinical trials, and medical records can be evaluated in the healthcare industry to progress medical research and enhance patient care. Unstructured data processing and analysis creates new opportunities for creativity and competitive advantage.

To utilize structured and unstructured data efficiently, companies must use various tools and technologies. Structured data management requires relational database management systems (RDBMS) and data warehousing solutions. Big data technologies like Hadoop and NoSQL databases like MongoDB and Cassandra offer the scalability and flexibility required to manage vast amounts of heterogeneous data regarding unstructured data. Furthermore, using machine learning and artificial intelligence is crucial in deriving insights from unstructured data using natural language processing, image identification, and audio analysis.

In conclusion, any data-driven business must comprehend the differences between structured and unstructured data as well as the sources of each. Because of its well-organized nature, structured data is perfect for typical data processing activities because it makes storage and analysis easier. Even though it requires sophisticated analytical methods and tools, unstructured data provides deeper insights and a more comprehensive viewpoint. Organizations may obtain complete insights, stimulate innovation, and sustain a competitive advantage in an increasingly data-centric world by efficiently managing and analyzing both kinds of data.

Common data sources: databases, APIs, web scraping, IoT devices

In the modern landscape of data science, harnessing and analyzing vast amounts of data from various sources is crucial for generating insights and making informed decisions. Familiar data sources include databases, APIs, web scraping, and IoT devices, each offering unique advantages and posing specific challenges. Understanding these sources is essential for effectively leveraging data in any analytical endeavor.

Databases are among the most traditional and widely used sources of data. They store structured data in a highly organized manner, typically within relational database management systems (RDBMS) like MySQL, PostgreSQL, and Oracle. These systems use Structured Query Language (SQL) to manage and manipulate data, making retrieving, updating, and analyzing information easy. Databases are integral to many business operations, storing critical data such as customer information, transaction records, and inventory levels. They ensure data integrity and consistency, which are vital for reliable analysis and reporting. Additionally, modern advancements have led to the development of NoSQL databases like MongoDB and Cassandra, designed to handle large volumes of unstructured or semi-structured data. These databases benefit applications requiring high scalability and flexibility, such as social media platforms and big data analytics.

APIs, or Application Programming Interfaces, are another significant data source. They allow different software applications to communicate and exchange data in a standardized way. APIs are especially useful for accessing real-time data from external services like financial markets, weather updates, social media, and more. For instance, a company might use APIs to integrate real-time stock prices into their economic analysis tools or to pull customer reviews from e-commerce platforms. APIs provide a seamless way to collect data without direct access to the source systems. However, working with APIs requires understanding their protocols and limitations, including rate limits, data formats (such as JSON or XML), and authentication methods. Properly managing API connections and ensuring data quality is crucial for leveraging this data source effectively.

Web scraping is a technique used to extract data from websites. This method involves writing scripts or using tools that automatically navigate web pages, identify relevant information, and extract it for analysis. Web scraping is particularly valuable for collecting data not readily available through APIs or databases. For example, businesses might scrape competitor prices, product reviews, or market trends from various online sources. Python libraries like BeautifulSoup and Scrapy are commonly used for web scraping, providing robust frameworks for parsing HTML and extracting data. While web scraping can yield rich datasets, it also comes with challenges. Websites often change their structure, requiring constant updates to scraping scripts. Additionally, ethical and legal considerations must be considered, as scraping can sometimes violate a website's terms of service or infringe on intellectual property rights.

Ensuring compliance with legal standards and handling data is essential when employing web scraping techniques.

The proliferation of IoT (Internet of Things) devices has introduced a new dimension to data collection, offering vast amounts of real-time, sensor-generated data. IoT devices range from simple household gadgets like smart thermostats and fitness trackers to complex industrial machines and smart city infrastructures. These devices continuously collect data on various parameters, such as temperature, humidity, motion, location, etc. The data from IoT devices is typically unstructured and requires significant preprocessing before analysis. Platforms like AWS IoT, Google Cloud IoT, and Microsoft Azure IoT provide the necessary infrastructure to collect, store, and process this data at scale. IoT data can offer valuable insights across numerous applications, from optimizing manufacturing processes and enhancing predictive maintenance to improving urban planning and environmental monitoring. However, managing IoT data involves addressing data volume, variety, velocity, and veracity challenges. Data security and privacy are also a significant concern, given the sensitive nature of information collected by many IoT devices.

In conclusion, familiar data sources such as databases, APIs, web scraping, and IoT devices contribute uniquely to the data landscape. Databases provide structured, reliable data crucial for many business operations, while APIs offer real-time data access from a wide range of external services. Web scraping enables extracting data from web pages, filling gaps where APIs are unavailable. IoT devices generate vast amounts of real-time data, offering new insights into physical environments and processes. Each data source presents distinct advantages and challenges, requiring specific tools, techniques, and considerations to harness their full potential. By effectively integrating and analyzing data from these diverse sources, organizations can enhance their decision-making processes, drive innovation, and maintain a competitive edge in the data-driven world. Understanding the nuances of these data sources is essential for any data scientist or analyst aiming to leverage data effectively in their work.

Ethical considerations and data privacy

Ethical considerations and data privacy have become paramount concerns in the era of big data and advanced analytics. As organizations increasingly rely on data to drive decision-making, the need to address ethical issues and ensure data privacy has never been more critical. Ethical considerations in data science encompass various issues, including consent, transparency, bias, and fairness. Data privacy protects individuals' personal information from unauthorized access and misuse. These aspects form the foundation for responsible data management practices that safeguard individual rights and promote trust in data-driven systems.

One of the primary ethical considerations in data science is obtaining informed consent from individuals whose data is being collected and analyzed. Consent implies that individuals are fully aware of what data is being collected, how it will be used, and who will have access to it. Without informed consent, individuals may feel their privacy violated, leading to mistrust in data practices, ensuring that consent is freely given, specific, informed, and unambiguous. It is essential in contexts involving sensitive personal information, such as health data or financial records. Organizations must be transparent about their data collection practices and provide clear, accessible information to individuals.

Transparency is another critical ethical consideration. It makes data practices open and understandable to all stakeholders, including data subjects, customers, and regulators. Transparency helps build trust and allows individuals to make informed decisions about their data. For instance, organizations should disclose how they collect, store, and use data and the measures they take to protect it. Transparency also explains the algorithms and models used in data analysis—Black-box models, where the opaque decision-making process can lead to suspicion and resistance. Explaining and justifying automated decisions helps demystify data processes and demonstrates accountability.

Bias and fairness in data analysis are significant ethical issues. Data-driven models and algorithms can inadvertently perpetuate and even exacerbate existing biases in the data. For example, suppose a hiring algorithm is trained on historical hiring data that reflects gender or racial biases. In that case, it may favor certain groups over others, leading to unfair outcomes. Ensuring fairness requires actively identifying and mitigating biases in data and algorithms. That involves using bias detection, fairness constraints, and diverse training data. Regular audits and assessments of data processes can help identify potential biases and ensure that data-driven decisions are equitable.

Data privacy is a fundamental aspect of ethical data management. It protects personal information from unauthorized access, use, disclosure, disruption, modification, or destruction. Data privacy is governed by various laws and regulations worldwide, such as the General Data Protection Regulation (GDPR) in the European Union and the California Consumer Privacy Act (CCPA) in the United States. These regulations set strict standards for handling personal data, emphasizing the importance of individual rights, such as the right to access, correct, and delete personal data. Compliance with these regulations is a legal obligation and an ethical imperative to respect individuals' privacy.

Implementing robust data security measures is crucial for safeguarding data privacy. These measures include technical measures such as encryption, anonymization, and access controls, and organizational measures like policies, training, and incident response plans. Encryption ensures that data is unreadable to unauthorized users, while anonymization removes personally identifiable information, reducing the risk of re-identification. Access controls limit who can view or manipulate data, ensuring only authorized personnel can access it. Regular security audits and vulnerability assessments can help identify and address potential weaknesses in data systems.

Another ethical consideration is the potential misuse of data. Data can be used to manipulate or exploit individuals in various ways, such as through targeted advertising, political propaganda, or social engineering. Organizations must be vigilant in preventing such misuse by implementing ethical guidelines and monitoring data use. They must ensure that data is used in ways consistent with the original purpose for which it was collected and that it does not harm individuals or society.

Ethical considerations and data privacy also extend to emerging technologies such as artificial intelligence (AI) and machine learning (ML). These technologies can potentially revolutionize many aspects of society but pose new ethical challenges. For example, AI systems can make decisions that significantly impact individuals' lives, such as healthcare, finance, and criminal justice. Ensuring that these systems are transparent, fair, and accountable is essential. It involves technical solutions, ethical oversight, and governance structures that can guide the responsible development and deployment of AI and ML technologies.

In conclusion, ethical considerations and data privacy are essential for responsible data management. They encompass various issues, from obtaining informed consent and ensuring transparency to addressing bias and protecting personal information. As data and advanced analytics use continue to grow, organizations must prioritize these ethical aspects to build trust, comply with regulations, and promote fair and equitable outcomes. By implementing robust data privacy measures and fostering an ethical data culture, organizations can harness the power of data while respecting individual rights and societal values.

Chapter V

Data Collection and Preprocessing

Techniques for data collection: surveys, experiments, scraping

As the cornerstone of analysis and insights, data gathering is essential in the research process. There are various methods for gathering data, and each has unique benefits and drawbacks. Three popular techniques that address multiple research needs and situations include web scraping, experiments, and surveys. Understanding these methods, their uses and the factors that need to be considered can significantly improve the caliber and dependability of the data gathered.

Surveys are one of the most common and versatile techniques for data collection. They involve asking a series of questions to a sample of individuals to gather information on their behaviors, opinions, attitudes, or characteristics. Surveys can be conducted in various formats, including online questionnaires, telephone interviews, face-to-face interviews, and mail surveys. The primary advantage of surveys is their ability to reach a large audience relatively quickly and cheaply, especially with the advent of online survey tools like SurveyMonkey, Google Forms, and Qualtrics. Surveys can be tailored to specific research objectives, allowing researchers to collect quantitative and qualitative data.

However, designing an effective survey requires careful consideration of several factors. The questions must be clear, unbiased, and relevant to the research goals. Poorly designed questions can lead to inaccurate or misleading responses. Additionally, sampling is crucial to ensure that the survey results represent the broader population. Techniques such as random, stratified, and cluster sampling can help achieve this. Response rates are another critical factor; low response rates can introduce bias, as those who choose to respond may differ significantly from those who do not. Ensuring anonymity, providing incentives, and simplifying the survey process can help improve response rates. Despite these challenges, surveys remain a powerful tool for collecting data across various fields, from market research to public health and social sciences.

Experiments are another essential technique for data collection, particularly in scientific research. Experiments involve manipulating one or more variables to observe the effect on another variable, allowing researchers to establish cause-and-effect relationships. This method is widely used in natural sciences, psychology, medicine, and social sciences. The primary strength of experiments lies in their ability to control for extraneous variables, thereby increasing the internal validity of the findings. By randomly assigning subjects to different conditions and preventing the experimental environment, researchers can isolate the effect of the independent variable on the dependent variable.

There are various types of experimental designs, including laboratory, field, and natural experiments. Laboratory experiments are conducted in controlled settings, which allows for precise manipulation of variables but may suffer from low external validity due to their artificial nature. Field experiments in real-world settings offer higher external validity but often at the expense of control over extraneous variables. Natural experiments take advantage of naturally occurring events to study their impact on a population, providing insights that would be difficult or unethical to obtain through deliberate manipulation. Despite their strengths, experiments can be resource-intensive and time-consuming. They also pose ethical considerations, especially when involving human subjects. Researchers must ensure their experiments are ethically sound, obtaining informed consent and minimizing potential harm to participants.

Web scraping is a modern technique for data collection that involves extracting information from websites. This method is beneficial for gathering large volumes of data from online sources, such as social media platforms, e-commerce sites, and news websites. Web scraping can be automated using tools and programming languages like Python, with libraries such as BeautifulSoup, Scrapy, and Selenium. These tools allow researchers to programmatically navigate web pages, extract relevant data, and store it in a structured format for analysis.

One of the main advantages of web scraping is its ability to collect real-time data on a large scale, which can be particularly valuable for trend analysis, market research, and sentiment analysis. However, web scraping also presents significant challenges and ethical considerations. Websites often change their structure, which can break scraping scripts and require continuous maintenance. Moreover, scraping can be legally and ethically contentious, as it may violate the terms of service of websites or infringe on intellectual property rights. Researchers must ensure that their scraping activities comply with legal standards and respect the data's privacy and ownership rights. Additionally, the quality and reliability of the data obtained through scraping can vary, necessitating thorough cleaning and validation processes to ensure its accuracy and usability.

Each data collection technique—surveys, experiments, and web scraping—has advantages and challenges, making them suitable for different research contexts and objectives. Surveys are ideal for gathering broad, self-reported data from a large audience, offering flexibility in question design and administration. Experiments provide a robust method for establishing causal relationships, with the trade-off between control and ecological validity depending on the type of experimental design. Web scraping offers a powerful way to collect vast amounts of real-time data from online sources, though it requires careful consideration of legal and ethical implications.

In conclusion, the choice of data collection technique depends on the specific research goals, the nature of the data required, and the resources available. By understanding the strengths and limitations of surveys, experiments, and web scraping, researchers can select the most appropriate method for their needs, ensuring the collection of high-quality, reliable data. This foundational step is critical for conducting rigorous analysis and deriving meaningful insights to inform decision-making and advance knowledge across various domains.

Data cleaning methods: handling missing values, outlier detection

Data cleaning, or data preparation, is the process of detecting and resolving mistakes, inconsistencies, and abnormalities in raw data to guarantee its quality and dependability. It is a crucial phase in the data science process. Outlier detection and handling missing values are two popular techniques for data cleansing. These techniques are essential for preparing data for analysis since outliers and missing values can distort results, jeopardize the validity of models, and produce incorrect conclusions. Ensuring the legitimacy and integrity of data-driven insights requires a thorough understanding of these techniques and their practical application.

Handling missing values is a fundamental aspect of data cleaning, as missing data is expected in real-world datasets. Missing values can arise for various reasons, including human error, equipment malfunction, or intentional omission. Regardless of the cause, missing values can introduce bias and reduce the effectiveness of analysis if not handled properly. There are several techniques for handling missing values, each with strengths and limitations. One approach is to remove observations or features with missing values entirely, known as complete case analysis or listwise deletion. While straightforward, this method can lead to a loss of valuable information, especially if missing values are prevalent. Another approach is imputation, which involves replacing missing values with estimated values based on other observations or statistical methods. Standard imputation techniques include mean imputation, median imputation, and regression imputation. Mean imputation replaces missing values with the mean of the observed values for that variable, while median imputation uses the median. Regression imputation involves predicting missing values using regression models based on other variables. Each imputation method has its assumptions and limitations, and researchers must carefully consider the implications of their choice on the analysis results.

Outlier detection is another essential data-cleaning method to identify and handle observations that deviate significantly from the rest of the data. Outliers can arise due to measurement errors, data entry mistakes, or genuine anomalies in the data generation process. Regardless of their origin, outliers can distort statistical analyses, bias parameter estimates, and undermine the performance of predictive models. Detecting outliers involves statistical techniques that quantify how observations deviate from the expected distribution. Standard methods for outlier detection include z-score, interquartile range (IQR), and isolation forests. The z-score method identifies outliers based on their deviation from the mean of the data distribution, where observations with z-scores beyond a certain threshold are considered outliers. The IQR method identifies outliers based on the difference between the third and first quartiles of the data distribution, where observations outside a specified range are flagged as outliers. Isolation forests are a machine learning-based method that uses decision trees to isolate outliers in high-dimensional data spaces. Once outliers are identified, researchers must decide how to handle them, which may involve removing, transforming, or treating them separately in the analysis.

While handling missing values and outlier detection are essential data-cleaning methods, they are not without challenges and considerations. One challenge is determining the appropriate threshold for identifying missing values and outliers. Setting thresholds too low may result in excessive data loss or the removal of genuine observations, while setting them too high may fail to detect significant anomalies. The data-cleaning method can also influence the analysis results and subsequent decision-making. Researchers must carefully consider the implications of their data-cleaning decisions on the validity and reliability of their findings. Moreover, data cleaning is an iterative process that often requires multiple rounds of inspection, cleaning, and validation to ensure that the data is suitable for analysis. Collaborating with domain experts and conducting sensitivity analyses can help validate data-cleaning decisions and mitigate potential biases or errors.

In conclusion, data cleaning methods such as handling missing values and outlier detection are essential for ensuring the quality and reliability of data in the data science process. Handling missing values involves identifying and replacing missing data with estimated values using techniques such as imputation. Outlier detection aims to identify and handle observations that deviate significantly from the rest of the data using statistical methods such as z-score and IQR. While these methods are crucial for preparing data for analysis, they require careful consideration of thresholds, assumptions, and implications for analysis results. By effectively understanding and implementing these data cleaning methods, researchers can ensure that their analyses are based on high-quality, reliable data, leading to more accurate insights and informed decision-making.

Data transformation techniques: normalization, encoding

Data transformation techniques are essential for preparing data for analysis. Allows data scientists to derive valuable insights and create precise predictive models. Normalization and encoding are popular data transformation methods with distinct uses and meet particular needs throughout the data preprocessing stage.

Numerical data can be rescaled using the normalization approach to a defined range, usually between 0 and 1 or -1 and 1. Normalization guarantees that each feature contributes equally to the analysis and keeps features with larger scales from predominating over those with more minor scales. When working with methods that are sensitive to the scale of the input features, such as gradient descent-based optimization algorithms used in machine learning, normalization is very crucial. Min-max scaling is a popular normalizing technique in which each feature is scaled to a given range according to its minimum and maximum values. Z-score normalization, or standardization, is an additional strategy that involves scaling each characteristic to have a mean of 0 and a standard deviation of 1. And ensure that machine learning algorithms catch patterns in the data efficiently and are not impacted by feature size, normalization is an essential preprocessing step that helps them perform better and converge faster.

Another crucial data transformation method for transforming categorical data into a numerical representation that machine learning algorithms can understand is encoding. Discrete categories or groups are represented by categorical data, frequently found in variables like gender, ethnicity, and product categories. Categorical variables must be encoded into a format that maintains their information while making them compatible with numerical computations, as most machine learning methods demand numerical input. A common technique for encoding categorical data is "one-hot encoding," and every category is represented by a binary vector whose length is the total number of distinct categories. Every category is given a particular binary value, where 0 denotes the category's absence, and 1 indicates its presence. The categorical variables are represented as a sparse matrix by one-hot encoding, making it appropriate for feeding into machine learning methods. Label encoding is an additional method for allocating an integer value to each category. Label encoding introduces ordinality when none exists, potentially confusing the algorithm, even though it is easier to use and requires less memory than one-hot encoding.

While encoding and normalizing are essential phases in data preprocessing, they are used for different things and on various kinds of data. Numerical features are mostly normalized to make sure they have equal magnitudes and are on a consistent scale. Normalization assures faster and more accurate convergence of machine learning algorithms by rescaling features to a standard range, preventing large-scale features from taking center stage in the study. Conversely, encoding is used to transform category information into a numerical representation that machine learning algorithms can handle. Encoding maintains the information of categorical variables and makes them compatible with numerical computations by representing them as numerical vectors. Normalization and encoding are necessary to prepare data for analysis and guarantee that machine learning models can successfully identify patterns and generate precise predictions.

In actuality, preparation procedures like feature selection and handling missing values are frequently used in conjunction with data transformation techniques like encoding and normalization. The dataset's particulars, the study's needs, and the employed algorithms all influence the selected transformation approaches. The effects of each modification on the analysis's findings and the model's interpretability must be carefully considered. Additionally, it is critical to test their efficacy using exploratory data analysis and cross-validation to ensure that data transformation strategies enhance the functionality and generalizability of machine learning models.

Data transformation methods like encoding and normalization are essential for preparing data for analysis and creating precise predictive models. Normalization rescales numerical data to a predefined range to ensure that every feature contributes equally to the analysis and to keep large-scale features from predominating over smaller ones. Encoding preserves the information in the categorical variables while making them compatible with numerical computations by converting categorical data into a numerical format that machine learning algorithms can process. Data scientists may guarantee that their analyses are founded on high-quality, standardized data by successfully implementing these transformation procedures, which will produce forecasts and insights that are more accurate.

CHAPTER VI

Exploratory Data Analysis (EDA)

Importance of EDA in data science

A fundamental stage in the data science process, exploratory data analysis (EDA), is essential to comprehending a dataset's underlying structure, trends, and relationships. To find patterns, spot irregularities, and create hypotheses—as well as to set the stage for more complex statistical analysis and modeling—EDA entails the analysis and visualization of data. It is impossible to overestimate the significance of EDA in data science since it offers insightful information on the properties of the data, directs choices made during further analysis, and aids in ensuring the accuracy and dependability of findings.

Acquiring a thorough grasp of the distribution and structure of the dataset is one of the main goals of EDA. Data scientists can determine a data distribution's form, dispersion, and central tendency by analyzing descriptive plots, histograms, and summary statistics. One must know these features to choose suitable statistical models and procedures and appropriately interpret the results. Furthermore, by using EDA, data scientists can find possible data quality problems, such as missing values, outliers, and inconsistencies, which may call for additional preparation before analysis.

Moreover, EDA is essential for identifying data links, patterns, and trends. Data scientists can investigate the relationships between variables, find correlations, and spot patterns that might not be immediately obvious from summary statistics alone by using visualizations like scatter plots, line charts, and heatmaps. Data scientists can use these insights to guide feature selection, hypothesis building, and model construction, creating more reliable and accurate predictive models. Furthermore, non-linear correlations and interactions between variables that would need more complex modeling techniques to represent successfully can be revealed by EDA.

Moreover, EDA is an essential tool for developing and validating hypotheses. Data scientists can create fresh concepts and insights into the underlying mechanisms behind the observed events by visually examining the data and testing different theories. ANOVA, chi-square, and t-tests are a few examples of hypothesis testing techniques that can assess whether observed associations or differences are statistically significant, hence supporting or contradicting theories. Additionally, EDA helps data scientists to iteratively improve their theories in light of fresh information and proof, which results in a deeper comprehension of the data and the phenomena under study.

Another crucial feature is the function that EDA plays in teamwork and communication. The EDA process produces visualizations helpful in sharing results and insights with stakeholders, subject matter experts, and other data science team members. Data visualizations facilitate discussions and decision-making by making intricate linkages and patterns easier to understand. Furthermore, EDA promotes collaboration and interdisciplinary discourse by offering a common language and structure for comprehending the data and its implications across many domains and expertise areas.

\EDA is vital for assuring the validity and dependability of outcomes in addition to its immediate advantages for analysis and decision-making. Data scientists can detect potential sources of bias, confounding variables, and other threats to validity that could affect the accuracy and generalizability of their conclusions by carefully examining the data and evaluating its quality. EDA also assists data scientists in assessing the underlying assumptions of their models and analysis methods to ensure they are suitable for the context and data. EDA helps reduce risks and uncertainties and improves the analysis's robustness and credibility by addressing these issues upfront.

To summarize, the data science process requires using exploratory data analysis or EDA. It offers insightful information on the organization, relationships, and patterns found in a dataset, which helps to inform further analytic choices and develop hypotheses. EDA assists data scientists in gaining a thorough knowledge of the data, identifying hidden patterns and relationships, and ensuring the validity and dependability of outcomes by looking at summary statistics, visualizing data, and testing hypotheses. Additionally, EDA promotes cooperation and communication by giving many stakeholders and areas of expertise a common language and structure for comprehending the data. In general, it is impossible to overestimate the significance of EDA in data science since it establishes the framework for sensible analysis, wise choices, and significant discoveries that spur advancement and creativity in various fields.

Techniques for EDA: visualization, summary statistics, pattern detection

The term "exploratory data analysis" (EDA) refers to a group of methods used to analyze and understand a dataset's properties, relationships, and organization. Pattern recognition, summary statistics, and visualization are three essential EDA approaches. These methods offer supplementary ways to comprehend the data, reveal latent patterns, and guide further analytical choices.

Data exploration and an intuitive understanding of the structure and relationships of the data are made possible by the potent visualization tool. Visualizations simplify and facilitate the interpretation of complicated patterns and trends by using graphics to illustrate the data. Common visualization approaches include heat maps, box plots, line charts, scatter plots, and histograms. While histograms and box plots offer information about the distribution and variability of a single variable, scatter plots are especially helpful for analyzing the relationship between two continuous variables. Heatmaps are useful for emphasizing patterns and correlations in multivariate data, whereas line charts help illustrate trends over time or across categories. Users can interactively examine data with interactive visualizations, like dynamic plots and interactive dashboards, which facilitate the development of deeper insights and hypotheses. In addition to aiding in identifying outliers, clusters, and patterns, visualization promotes cooperation and communication by giving many stakeholders and areas of expertise a common vocabulary and framework for comprehending the data.

Measures of central tendency, dispersion, and form are just a few examples of the essential aspects of the data that are quantitatively summarized by summary statistics. The mean, median, mode, standard deviation, variance, range, and percentiles are examples of standard summary statistics. Data scientists can better grasp the overall distribution and variability of the data by using these statistics, which offer insights into the typical value, spread, and variability of the data. Summary statistics are essential for identifying potential issues with data quality, such as missing values, outliers, and discrepancies, which may necessitate more investigation and preparation before analysis. Additionally, summary statistics make it possible to compare various groups or categories within the data, highlighting similarities and differences that guide further analytic choices. Although summary statistics offer a helpful synopsis of the data, they should be carefully understood and reinforced by visualizations to guarantee a thorough comprehension of the features of the data.

Pattern identification is identifying patterns, trends, and relationships in the data using statistical techniques and machine learning algorithms. These methods will likely reveal linkages and hidden structures that might not be readily clear from summary data or visualizations alone. Regression, association rule mining, clustering, and classification are standard pattern identification methods. By grouping related observations according to specific criteria, clustering techniques like K-means and hierarchical clustering expose underlying patterns and structures in the data. Regression and classification approaches help data scientists find patterns and relationships by predicting continuous or categorical outcomes based on input variables. Co-occurring patterns or correlations between variables are found by association rule mining; examples include market basket analysis in retail and customer segmentation in marketing. Pattern detection techniques complement visualization and summary statistics by providing a deeper understanding of the underlying structures and relationships within the data, enabling more informed analysis decisions and hypothesis generation.

In conclusion, methods for Exploratory Data Analysis (EDA) are crucial for understanding a dataset's composition, traits, and connections. These methods include visualization, summary statistics, and pattern recognition. Data is presented in an understandable graphical format through visualization, facilitating the interpretation and accessibility of intricate patterns and trends. In addition to facilitating comparisons across various groups or categories, summary statistics provide quantitative summaries of essential data features that may be used to indicate any problems with data quality.

By discovering hidden trends, patterns, and correlations within the data, pattern detection techniques offer deeper insights into the underlying associations and structures of the data. Effective use of these methods allows data scientists to fully comprehend the data, guide decisions made during subsequent analyses, and unearth insightful information that spurs innovation and advancement in various fields.

Tools for EDA: Python (Pandas, Matplotlib, Seaborn), R

Exploratory data analysis (EDA) is an important phase in the data science process, and efficiently exploring and visualizing data requires the use of the appropriate tools. Python and R are two popular programming languages for EDA, with a robust ecosystem of tools and packages made especially for data processing, visualization, and analysis in each language.

Python's versatility, ease of use, and rich library support have made it one of the most widely used programming languages for data research. Pandas, which offers high-performance data structures and data manipulation and analysis capabilities, is one of the essential libraries for EDA in Python. Pandas make it simple for data scientists to load, clean, filter, and transform data, making it ideal for exploratory analysis tasks. Grouping, averaging, and merging datasets are just a few problematic data operations that users can easily do with Pandas because of its robust capabilities and syntax. Furthermore, Pandas's data analysis and visualization capabilities are further enhanced by its smooth integration with other Python libraries, like NumPy and Matplotlib.

Apart from Pandas, two well-liked Python libraries for data visualization are Matplotlib and Seaborn, which offer an extensive selection of plotting functions and styles to produce informative visualizations. A low-level interface for generating a range of plots, such as line, scatter, and bar charts, is provided by the extensive plotting package Matplotlib. Even while Matplotlib offers a lot of customization and versatility, it may occasionally take a lot of work to use, particularly when making intricate visualizations or interactive plots. In contrast, Seaborn is based on Matplotlib and offers a more advanced interface for creating visually appealing and educational statistical visualizations. Along with providing more features for examining correlations between variables and visualizing distributions, Seaborn streamlines the process of constructing standard plots, like heatmaps, pair plots, and violin plots.

However, because of its robust built-in functions and broad library support, statisticians and data analysts have traditionally preferred the statistical programming language R. R for EDA's ecosystem of specialized packages created especially for data analysis and visualization is one of its key advantages. For example, the tidyverse is a group of R tools that make data management and visualization easier, such as dplyr, ggplot2, and tidyr. For data processing activities, including filtering, summarizing, and merging datasets, dplyr offers a set of user-friendly methods. Meanwhile, ggplot2 provides a grammar of graphics approach for producing complex and configurable charts. These tools allow data scientists to carry out intricate R EDA operations effectively and efficiently.

R has a vast array of domain-specific packages for specialized analysis tasks in addition to the tidy verse. For instance, the Shiny package enables users to develop interactive web applications for data exploration and insight sharing. In contrast, the Caret package offers a single interface for training and assessing machine learning models. The R package ecosystem is constantly changing as new functions and packages are created to meet new trends and problems in data science.

Although R and Python provide vital EDA tools, the decision between them frequently comes down to individual preferences, experience level, and the analysis assignment's particulars. Python is well-known for its general-purpose programming abilities, and data scientists who appreciate adaptability and versatility choose it. R, on the other hand, provides a more unified and integrated environment for EDA activities and is highly specialized for statistical analysis. The optimal EDA tool lets data scientists analyze and display data quickly and effectively regardless of the programming language. Data scientists can obtain essential insights, find hidden patterns, and make well-informed decisions that spur innovation and advancement in their respective professions by utilizing the rich ecosystems of R and Python.

CHAPTER VII

Statistical Analysis and Inference

Fundamental concepts of statistics relevant to data science

As the theoretical underpinning and analytical tools required for comprehending and interpreting data, statistics is a fundamental field in data science. Several core statistics ideas are especially pertinent to data science, influencing how data is gathered, examined, and interpreted to derive significant insights and arrive at defensible conclusions. These ideas, essential to the data science process, include probability theory, descriptive statistics, inferential statistics, and hypothesis testing.

Statistical inference is based on probability theory, which offers a framework for calculating uncertainty and unpredictability in data. Probability quantifies the possibility that various results from a particular experiment or event will occur. Probability theory is used in data science to evaluate risk, model uncertainty, and create data-driven predictions. Understanding the underlying unpredictability and uncertainty in data requires a foundational understanding of concepts like conditional probability, random variables, and probability distributions. Probability theory allows data scientists to quantify uncertainty and make data-driven decisions by enabling them to formulate probabilistic assertions about the chance of particular occurrences or outcomes occurring.

A dataset's fundamental characteristics are described using descriptive statistics, revealing information about the dataset's distribution, dispersion, and central tendency. Measures like mean, median, mode, variance, and standard deviation are examples of descriptive statistics that give a succinct description of the properties of the data. Data scientists can detect outliers and anomalies, comprehend the general structure and trends, and depict the data using graphical representations like scatter plots, box plots, and histograms using descriptive statistics. Descriptive statistics help data scientists understand the underlying patterns and relationships in the data by summarizing its salient elements. This knowledge informs further analysis and interpretation of the data.

Sample data and inferential statistics go beyond descriptive statistics to infer and conclude about populations. Data scientists can extrapolate results from a sample to a larger population with inferential statistics, which employ estimation methods, confidence intervals, and hypothesis testing. A key idea in inferential statistics is hypothesis testing, which involves developing and evaluating hypotheses regarding population parameters using sample data. Data scientists can determine the validity of hypotheses and the importance of results by comparing observed data to predicted outcomes under a null hypothesis. It allows them to assess the likelihood of witnessing the data if the null hypothesis were true. Given the inherent uncertainty in predicting population features from sample data, confidence intervals offer a range of reasonable values for population attributes. Data scientists can estimate unknown parameters and make predictions based on data by using estimation techniques like maximum likelihood estimation and Bayesian inference.

A key idea in inferential statistics is hypothesis testing, which involves developing and evaluating hypotheses regarding population parameters using sample data. Data scientists can determine the validity of hypotheses and the importance of results by comparing observed data to predicted outcomes under a null hypothesis. That allows them to assess the likelihood of witnessing the data if the null hypothesis were true. Given the inherent uncertainty in predicting population features from sample data, confidence intervals offer a range of reasonable values for population attributes. Data scientists can estimate unknown parameters and make predictions based on data by using estimation techniques like maximum likelihood estimation and Bayesian inference.

The theoretical underpinnings of data science are these core statistical ideas, which influence the methods used to gather, examine, and interpret data to derive valuable insights and make defensible conclusions. Data scientists can quantify uncertainty, summarize data attributes, draw conclusions about populations, and test hypotheses using sample data by utilizing probability theory, descriptive statistics, inferential statistics, and hypothesis testing. These ideas are the cornerstone of statistical thinking in data science, directing all aspects of data analysis, from gathering and interpreting data to making decisions. Anybody working in the field of data science must have a firm grasp of these foundational statistical ideas to extract valuable insights from data and promote innovation and advancement across various sectors in the age of big data and advanced analytics.

Hypothesis testing, confidence intervals, regression analysis

In statistics, several fundamental tools are pivotal in analyzing data, drawing conclusions, and making predictions. Three such tools are hypothesis testing, confidence intervals, and regression analysis. Each serves distinct purposes but collectively contributes to the robustness of statistical analysis.

Hypothesis testing is a cornerstone of inferential statistics, providing a framework for making decisions based on sample data regarding the population parameter. At its core, hypothesis testing involves formulating two competing hypotheses: the null hypothesis (H0) and the alternative hypothesis (H1). The null hypothesis represents the status quo or the absence of an effect, while the alternative hypothesis suggests the presence of an impact or a difference. By collecting sample data and assessing the likelihood of observing such data if the null hypothesis were true, statisticians can determine whether to accept or reject the null hypothesis.

Confidence intervals offer a complementary approach to hypothesis testing, providing a range of plausible values for a population parameter and an associated confidence level. Unlike hypothesis testing, which focuses on accepting or rejecting a specific hypothesis, confidence intervals provide a more nuanced understanding of the uncertainty surrounding an estimate. Typically, a confidence interval is constructed using sample data and the sampling distribution of a statistic, such as the sample mean or proportion. The width of the interval is determined by factors such as the sample size and the chosen confidence level. By interpreting the confidence interval, analysts can assess their estimates' precision and gauge their conclusions' reliability.

Regression analysis encompasses a broad set of statistical methods aimed at modeling the relationship between one or more independent variables and a dependent variable. At its simplest, regression analysis seeks to fit a mathematical model to observed data, allowing researchers to explore and quantify the association between variables. Linear regression, the most well-known regression analysis, assumes a linear relationship between the independent and dependent variables. By estimating the parameters of the regression model, such as the slope and intercept, analysts can make predictions and infer causal relationships between variables.

Regression analysis is widely used across various disciplines, from economics and epidemiology to psychology and engineering, owing to its versatility and interpretability.

While distinct in their methodologies, these statistical tools are often interconnected and complementary in practice. For instance, hypothesis testing can evaluate the significance of coefficients in a regression model, while confidence intervals can provide insights into the precision of those estimates. Moreover, regression analysis can serve as a tool for hypothesis testing by examining whether the coefficients of independent variables differ significantly from zero. By leveraging these tools, analysts can gain a more comprehensive understanding of the data and draw more robust conclusions.

In conclusion, hypothesis testing, confidence intervals, and regression analysis are essential components of the statistical toolkit, enabling researchers to infer population parameters, quantify uncertainty, and model relationships between variables. While each tool has its unique strengths and applications, their combined use enhances the rigor and validity of statistical analysis. Whether investigating the effectiveness of a new treatment, forecasting future trends, or uncovering patterns in complex datasets, these statistical methods provide invaluable insights into the underlying phenomena and inform evidence-based decision-making.

Software tools: R, Python (SciPy, StatsModels)

Software tools play a critical role in converting unprocessed data into meaningful insights in data science and statistical analysis. R and Python are well-known tools in this field, providing a vast ecosystem of packages and modules designed specifically for machine learning, data visualization, and statistical modeling. The SciPy and StatsModels packages substantially improve scientific computing and statistical analysis capabilities within the Python ecosystem. These software tools enable researchers, analysts, and data scientists to examine, analyze, and interpret complex datasets efficiently and precisely.

R, an open-source programming language and environment designed explicitly for statistical computing and graphics, has gained widespread popularity among statisticians and data analysts. With its extensive collection of packages, including "ggplot2" for data visualization and "dplyr" for data manipulation, R provides a comprehensive suite of tools for exploratory data analysis and statistical modeling. Its syntax, optimized for statistical tasks, enables users to express complex analytical procedures concisely and intuitively. Moreover, R's vibrant community fosters collaboration and knowledge-sharing, with countless resources and tutorials supporting users at all skill levels.

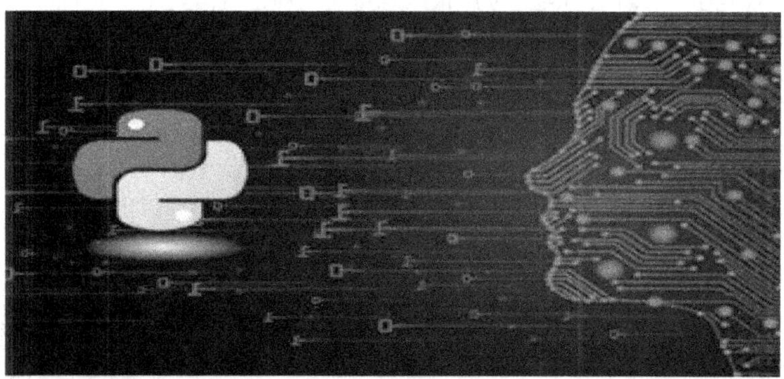

On the other hand, Python, a general-purpose programming language renowned for its versatility and readability, has emerged as a dominant force in data science. While Python's standard library includes essential statistical functions, its true power lies in its ecosystem of third-party libraries, such as NumPy, Pandas, SciPy, and StatsModels. NumPy provides critical tools for numerical computing, while Pandas offers high-level data structures and functions for data manipulation and analysis. SciPy extends Python's capabilities with modules for optimization, integration, interpolation, and other scientific computations, making it a valuable asset for researchers and engineers. Meanwhile, StatsModels specializes in econometrics and statistical modeling, offering various methods for regression analysis, time series analysis, and hypothesis testing.

Integrating SciPy and StatsModels into the Python ecosystem further elevates Python's capabilities for scientific computing and statistical analysis. SciPy's modules, such as "scipy. stats" for probability distributions and hypothesis tests, complement StatsModels' regression models and statistical tests, enabling users to perform advanced analyses efficiently. Moreover, Python's versatility extends beyond statistical analysis, with libraries like "scikit-learn" for machine learning, "Matplotlib" for data visualization, and "TensorFlow" for deep learning, making it a preferred choice for end-to-end data science projects.

Despite their differences, R and Python share a common goal: to empower users with the tools and resources needed to extract meaningful insights from data. While R excels in statistical computing and visualization, Python offers a broader ecosystem and greater flexibility for diverse applications. Consequently, the choice between R and Python often depends on personal preference, project requirements, and specific tasks. Some analysts may prefer the simplicity and elegance of R's syntax, while others may gravitate towards Python's versatility and extensive libraries.

To sum up, R and Python and their corresponding libraries, like SciPy and StatsModels, are the cornerstones of contemporary data science, empowering practitioners to confidently and accurately take on challenging analytical problems. These software programs offer the fundamental building blocks for statistical analysis and scientific investigation, whether used for testing hypotheses, fitting regression models, or looking for patterns in data. Researchers, analysts, and data scientists can drive informed decision-making in an increasingly data-driven environment by fully utilizing their data using R, Python, and related frameworks.

CHAPTER VIII

Machine Learning Basics

Introduction to machine learning and its significance

AI's machine learning (ML) subset has transformed several industries by allowing computers to learn from data and make judgments with little human input. Its importance comes from its vast range of applications that impact our daily lives and its technical prowess. Understanding machine learning fundamentals entails exploring its kinds, definitions, underlying algorithms, and broad applications.

The definition of machine learning is a data analysis technique that automates the creation of analytical models. It is predicated on the idea that machines can learn from data, spot patterns, and make judgments with little help from humans. It has undergone substantial change since Arthur Samuel first used the word in 1959. These days, machine learning is a vital part of artificial intelligence (AI), allowing systems to grow and change over time without requiring explicit programming for each task.

The primary forms of machine learning are supervised, unsupervised, semi-supervised, and reinforcement learning. A labeled dataset is used for supervised learning, meaning every training example has an output label. This kind is usually applied to jobs involving regression and classification, where the model is trained to forecast results based on input data. Examples include identifying spam in emails and forecasting real estate values.

Conversely, unsupervised learning works with unlabeled data. Without specific guidance on what to anticipate, the system attempts to infer the underlying structure from the input data. Unsupervised learning frequently involves tasks like association and clustering. For example, companies utilize clustering to categorize customers based on their purchase patterns without the customers' prior knowledge. This process is known as customer segmentation.

A combination of supervised and unsupervised learning is known as semi-supervised learning. It uses a massive amount of unlabeled data and a small amount of annotated data to train models. When classifying data is costly or time-consuming, this method can be helpful. Unlike other learning methods, reinforcement learning teaches an agent to make a series of decisions by rewarding and punishing good behavior. It is extensively utilized in autonomous driving, gaming, and robotics.

A multitude of different algorithms powers these different learning kinds. Standard techniques in supervised learning include support vector machines (SVM), decision trees, neural networks, logistic regression, and linear regression. For instance, logistic regression is utilized for binary classification issues, whereas linear regression predicts continuous outcomes. Because of their interpretability and versatility, decision trees and SVMs are employed for regression and classification problems. Inspired by the architecture of the human brain, neural networks play a crucial role in deep learning, a branch of machine learning that manages complex tasks like speech and picture recognition.

Principal component analysis (PCA), hierarchical clustering, and k-means clustering are examples of unsupervised learning techniques. K-means clustering separates data into k unique clusters based on feature similarity, while hierarchical clustering produces a tree of clusters, allowing for a more detailed grouping of data. By lowering the number of variables being examined, PCA is a dimensionality reduction approach that simplifies data and makes it simpler to view and analyze.

Algorithms like deep Q-networks (DQN) and Q-learning are widely used in reinforcement learning. Q-learning is a model-free technique that aims to determine the worth of an action in a specific state to assist the agent in making the best decisions. By adding neural networks, DQNs expand on Q-learning and enable agents to operate in more complicated situations.

It is impossible to overestimate the importance of machine learning in the modern world. Its ability to solve complicated problems in a more scalable, accurate, and efficient manner has revolutionized several industries. For instance, machine learning models are used in healthcare to speed up drug discovery, customize treatment regimens, and forecast disease outbreaks. These algorithms can uncover patterns in massive volumes of medical data frequently invisible to human physicians, resulting in earlier diagnoses and better patient outcomes.

Machine learning is utilized in the financial industry for personalized banking, fraud detection, credit scoring, and algorithmic trading. Machine learning algorithms can make real-time trading judgments, frequently surpassing human traders, by examining past data and market trends. Credit scoring models help lenders make better judgments by assessing the probability that a borrower would default. Fraud detection systems offer extra protection by using machine learning to spot odd trends that might point to fraudulent activity.

E-commerce platforms use machine learning for customer support, inventory control, and recommendation systems. Recommendation engines analyze user behavior and preferences to make product recommendations that improve the shopping experience and increase revenue. Models for inventory management anticipate consumer demand, resulting in ideal stock levels and lower expenses. Machine learning-powered chatbots and virtual assistants offer immediate client responses, increasing service satisfaction and efficiency.

Machine learning algorithms are used in social media to personalize content streams, identify inappropriate information, and enable targeted advertising. These algorithms examine user interactions to select material that will engage each user and keep them on the platform longer. To keep the internet a safer place, content moderation systems utilize machine learning to recognize and delete offensive or dangerous information. Machine learning helps advertisers by giving consumers more relevant ads, which enhances both the user experience and ad effectiveness.

The transportation industry also benefits from machine learning through autonomous vehicles, predictive maintenance, and traffic management. Autonomous learning by predicting compo to interpret sensory data, make driving judgments, and navigate challenging surroundings failures, predictive maintenance models lower maintenance costs and downtime by analyzing data from vehicle sensors. Traffic management systems use machine learning to maximize traffic flow, lessen congestion, and enhance safety.

To sum up, machine learning is a revolutionary technology with enormous promise. It is extremely helpful in a variety of industries due to its capacity to learn from data and improve over time without explicit programming. If we have a fundamental understanding of machine learning's kinds, methods, and applications, we can better grasp its relevance and tremendous impact on our world. Machine learning is expected to revolutionize our lives and work in the future as its applications grow and develop.

Types of machine learning: supervised, unsupervised, reinforcement learning

A branch of AI, machine learning (ML), is concerned with teaching computers to carry out tasks without human guidance through predefined algorithms and statistical models. Alternatively, these systems can learn from data and gradually become more efficient. The three primary schools of thought in machine learning are reinforcement, supervised, and unsupervised learning. Different types are best suited to tackle various issues and activities because of their qualities, approaches, and applications.

Supervised learning is perhaps the most common and widely used form of machine learning. It involves training a model on a labeled dataset, meaning each training example is paired with an output label. The primary goal of supervised learning is to learn a mapping from inputs to outputs, allowing the model to predict the label for new, unseen data. This learning process typically involves two main tasks: classification and regression. Classification is used when the output is a discrete label, such as determining whether an email is spam. Conversely, regression is used for continuous outputs, such as predicting house prices based on various features like location, size, and age.

Collecting a labeled dataset and dividing it into training and testing sets is the first step in supervised learning. During training, the model learns to link inputs with their respective labels in the training set. At this stage, the model tweaks its settings to reduce discrepancies between its forecasts and the accurate labels. After complete training, the model is tested on the testing set to see how well it applies to fresh data. Linear and logistic regression, decision trees, support vector machines (SVMs), and neural networks are some of the most popular algorithms used in supervised learning. The strengths and drawbacks of each algorithm dictate the problems and datasets they excel at solving.

Unsupervised learning is concerned with not labeled data, in contrast to supervised learning. Finding hidden patterns and structures in the data without labels is the objective. Exploratory data analysis, which seeks to reveal previously unseen connections and insights, is an ideal application of this kind of learning. The two main activities in unsupervised learning are association and clustering. The goal of clustering is to combine data items with similar characteristics. For instance, unsupervised learning can help separate groups of buyers who share common traits when it comes to client segmentation. Some popular clustering algorithms are DBSCAN (Density-Based Spatial Clustering of Applications with Noise), hierarchical clustering, and k-means clustering.

Finding intriguing correlations between variables in massive datasets is the goal of the association, the second primary objective of unsupervised learning. Market basket analysis is a famous example of an association-based application; this method seeks to determine which products buyers are most likely to buy together. Using this data, you may fine-tune your product positioning and upsell tactics. Association rule mining algorithms like Apriori and Eclat are widely used, allowing companies to make better data-based decisions.

A third branch of machine learning, reinforcement learning, draws inspiration from behavioral psychology. Through repeated exposure to a specific setting, an agent is taught to make a predetermined set of decisions. In response to its behaviors, the agent learns to optimize its cumulative rewards by receiving rewards or penalties. Reinforcement learning is based on the principle of trial and error to find the best actions, as opposed to supervised learning, which involves providing the proper response for every input.

Determining a reward function, an action space, and a state space are common steps in reinforcement learning. The agent takes stock of its surroundings, decides what to do in response to that knowledge, and then moves on to the next state while collecting its reward. Ultimately, the goal of the agent's learning process should be to maximize the total reward. Policy gradient techniques, Q-learning, and deep Q-networks (DQN) are essential algorithms in reinforcement learning.

Q-learning, a model-free method, attempts to learn the worth of a specific action in a particular state to aid the agent in making the best possible decisions. To better manage complicated situations with high-dimensional state spaces, deep Q-networks use neural networks, expanding Q-learning. In contrast, policy gradient approaches optimize the policy directly by shifting its parameters to maximize predicted benefits. Many fields have succeeded with reinforcement learning applications, such as robotics, gaming, and autonomous driving.

Each of the three main branches of machine learning has several uses and advantages: supervised, unsupervised, and reinforcement learning. Email filtering, medical diagnosis, and financial forecasting are just a few examples of supervised learning's optimal uses, as it thrives in predictive tasks with abundant labeled data. Unsupervised learning excels at exploratory data analysis by revealing latent structures and patterns in domains such as consumer segmentation and anomaly detection, where labeled data is scarce. Autonomous navigation, industrial automation, and strategic game-playing are examples of the adaptive strategy domains where reinforcement learning's emphasis on sequential decision-making has proven highly effective.

It is essential to grasp the various machine learning approaches well to choose the best method for any given situation. Using suitable machine learning approaches, we can create intelligent systems that use data to make better decisions, work faster, and open up new opportunities in many different areas. The more machine learning develops, the more things it can do, and the more it will change how we perceive and engage with the world.

Key algorithms: regression, classification, clustering, neural networks

An essential part of AI, machine learning uses various algorithms to autonomously examine data, learn from it, and then make predictions or judgments about the future. Algorithms like neural networks, clustering, classification, and regression stand out because of their adaptability and wide-ranging uses. You need to know these essential algorithms to use machine learning in all contexts.

The foundation of numerous predictive modeling jobs is regression algorithms. You can use them to predict continuous outcomes by modeling the link between a dependent variable and one or more independent variables. Linear regression is the most basic kind because it takes the input variables and outputs as given and presumes that the connection is linear. The main goal is to locate the best line that fits the data by minimizing the sum of squared discrepancies between the predicted and observed values. Housing price predictions using location, size, and condition are just a few examples of the many applications of linear regression in the social sciences, economics, and finance.

Multivariate and polynomial regression, two more advanced types, deal with non-linear relationships and multiple input variables, respectively. By fitting a polynomial equation to the data, polynomial regression can capture more nuanced patterns. Numerous independent variables, an extension of linear regression, can allow for a more thorough examination of the factors impacting the dependent variable. Businesses and researchers rely on regression algorithms, essential data science tools, to find trends, make forecasts, and guide decision-making.

Contrary to regression, classification algorithms handle results that fall into predetermined categories. The objective is to sort the supplied data into predetermined categories. For binary classification problems with a possible output of one of two classes, logistic regression is a simple approach that can be utilized. Despite its name, logistic regression is a classification algorithm that employs the logistic function to represent the probability of a specific class. Healthcare, marketing, and finance are just a few industries that heavily use it for disease detection and consumer segmentation.

Decision trees, support vector machines (SVMs), and k-nearest neighbors (KNNs) are more complex classification techniques than logistic regression. Decision trees create a decision-making model in the shape of a tree by partitioning the data into subsets according to the importance of input features. From medical diagnosis to fraud detection, this method's straightforward and easily interpretable nature makes it suitable for various applications. In contrast, support vector machines (SVMs) use a high-dimensional space to locate the best hyperplane for classifying data points. Image recognition and bioinformatics are two areas that use their high dimensionality well. KNN is a simple and effective classifier for handwriting recognition and recommendation systems. It uses the majority class among its k-nearest neighbors in the feature space to classify data points.

One form of unsupervised learning, clustering algorithms seek to group comparable data points without specified labels. Exploratory data analysis relies heavily on these techniques to unearth latent structures and patterns in the data. When it comes to clustering algorithms, K-means is among the most used. Each data point is placed in the cluster with the nearest mean after the data is partitioned into k clusters. Efficient and straightforward to build, the approach refines the cluster centroids iteratively until convergence. Anomaly detection, picture compression, and market segmentation are some of the many applications of K-means.

Another well-known technique, hierarchical clustering, constructs a cluster tree using agglomerative (bottom-up) or divisive (top-down) methods. A dendrogram, a diagram similar to a tree, showing the clusters' arrangement is produced by this method; the number of clusters to be used is not determined in advance. Many scientific disciplines find hierarchical clustering useful, including biology for building phylogenetic trees and social network analysis. A more sophisticated clustering technique, DBSCAN (Density-Based Spatial Clustering of Applications with Noise), groups data points according to their density, successfully detecting clusters of any shape and dealing with data noise. It shines when applied to data mining and geographical analysis.

When it comes to jobs containing complicated data, neural networks—modeled after how the human brain works—have completely changed the game for machine learning. Layers of interconnected "neurons," or nodes, with the ability to execute basic computations, make up a neural network. Backpropagation is how the network learns from its mistakes by modifying the connection weights. Deep learning, a branch of machine learning, is based on neural networks and is very good at processing massive amounts of unstructured data, including text, audio, and pictures.

When it comes to processing input that is grid-like, like photographs, convolutional neural networks (CNNs) are the way to go. Image classification, object detection, and face recognition are just a few of the many applications of convolutional layers. These algorithms learn spatial feature hierarchies automatically and adaptively. Another kind, recurrent neural networks (RNNs), are also designed to handle sequential data, such as time series and natural language. For applications like language modeling and speech recognition, RNNs' architecture includes loops that let them retain a memory of prior inputs.

From medical imaging and medication development in healthcare to recommendation systems and content generation in entertainment, neural networks have made tremendous progress across diverse domains. They are extremely useful for tasks that conventional algorithms find difficult to model because they can represent complicated, non-linear relationships.

Finally, some of the most essential algorithms in machine learning are neural networks, clustering, classification, and regression. Predictive models rely on regression and classification, which allow for the prediction of continuous outcomes and data classification into preset classes. Regarding exploratory data analysis, clustering algorithms are masters in revealing latent patterns in unlabeled data. Advancements in image and audio recognition, natural language processing, and other domains have been propelled by neural networks, which can learn complex patterns from massive volumes of data. If we want to use machine learning to its maximum capacity, which can lead to innovations and better decisions in many different sectors, we must master these algorithms.

CHAPTER IX

Advanced Machine Learning Techniques

Deep learning and neural networks

Some of the most cutting-edge and game-changing methods in machine learning, such as deep learning and neural networks, have emerged in the last several decades. These methods have profoundly affected many fields, including autonomous systems, natural language processing, picture and audio recognition, and many more. Familiarity with these concepts is crucial for a full appreciation of the far-reaching effects and endless possibilities of deep learning and neural networks.

A subfield of machine learning, deep learning is concerned with multi-layered neural networks. The idea behind these networks is to make them act more like how our brains learn and see patterns. Unlike more conventional machine learning methods, deep learning may automatically learn representations from data without requiring human intervention in the form of feature extraction. Deep learning algorithms can now handle complicated, high-dimensional data, opening up new possibilities for previously impossible jobs.

Artificial neural networks, made up of layers of interconnected neurons, are the building blocks of deep learning. Each neuron receives input, processes it through an activation function, and sends the output to the next layer. Data flows in a single direction from the input layer to the output layer in a feedforward network, the simplest type of neural network. In train neural networks, a technique called backpropagation is employed to alter the weights of the neuronal connections to decrease the prediction error. This iterative procedure updates the weights using optimization algorithms like gradient descent to increase the network's performance.

For grid-like data like photographs, convolutional neural networks (CNNs) are the way to go. Convolutional neural networks (CNNs) capture feature hierarchies through convolutional layers that apply filters to input data. Thanks to their architecture, image categorization, object detection, and face recognition are just a few of the many applications that greatly benefit from CNNs' ability to discern complicated patterns—like edges, textures, and shapes. Medical imaging, autonomous driving, and security are just a few areas that have embraced CNNs due to their performance in image-related tasks.

One more kind of neural network that excels at processing time series and natural language sequences is the recurrent neural network (RNN). Recurrent Neural Networks (RNNs) can remember past inputs because of the architectural loops that distinguish them from feedforward networks. Language modeling, voice recognition, and machine translation are just a few applications where this functionality is vital. Unfortunately, training lengthy sequences with typical RNNs is difficult due to restrictions such as the vanishing gradient problem. Modern architectures such as the Gated Recurrent Unit (GRU) and the Long Short-Term Memory (LSTM) were created to solve this problem. These designs enhance RNN performance on complicated sequential tasks by using techniques to maintain long-term dependency.

Natural language processing (NLP) has significantly benefited from deep learning's capacity to analyze and gain knowledge from massive datasets. Models' capacity to comprehend and produce natural language has been improved by word embeddings, which store words in continuous vector space. When capturing word semantic links, models such as Word2Vec and GloVe have proved helpful. New developments in natural language processing have been made possible by transformer-based models such as GPT (Generative Pre-trained Transformer) and BERT (Bidirectional Encoder Representations from Transformers), which expand upon these earlier advancements. By using attention processes to scan whole sentences or paragraphs, these models improve context capturing and make possible incredibly accurate tasks like sentiment analysis, language translation, and text generation.

Creating generative models, including Variational Autoencoders (VAEs) and Generative Adversarial Networks (GANs), is another critical step forward in deep learning. A GAN's generator and discriminator neural networks compete with one another. While the discriminator verifies the validity of the data, the generator makes it up from scratch. Applications in image synthesis, video production, and drug discovery are made possible by this adversarial approach that generates exceedingly realistic data. In contrast, VAEs enable data compression, denoising, and anomaly detection by encoding incoming data into a lower-dimensional latent space and decoding it back to the original space.

Beyond their immediate practical uses, deep learning and neural networks will have far-reaching consequences for society. Deep learning models have proven beneficial in healthcare, where they aid in disease diagnosis, outcome prediction, and treatment plan personalization. These models can improve patient care and medical research by evaluating genetic data, electronic health records, and medical imaging to find patterns and correlations humans overlook. Deep learning is the brains behind autonomous vehicles in the car business. It lets them see their surroundings, decide what to do, and find their way around securely. This technology has the potential to alleviate traffic congestion, improve road safety, and open up new avenues of mobility for those with impairments.

Nevertheless, there are both practical and ethical concerns that arise from the fast development of deep learning. Concerns about deep learning models' interpretability and openness are substantial. Since these models are typically "black boxes," how they judge is not always clear; this absence of interpretability might pose a severe challenge in mission-critical domains where comprehending the logic underlying forecasts, such as healthcare and finance, is paramount. Researchers are actively working on approaches to make them more interpretable and explainable to ensure the responsible and trustworthy deployment of deep learning models.

Another obstacle is the need for substantial quantities of tagged data and processing resources. Powerful hardware, such as GPUs and TPUs, and considerable energy usage are sometimes required for the resource-intensive process of training deep learning models. Due to this necessity, small businesses and researchers with low resources may find deep learning technologies less accessible. Researchers are working on more efficient algorithms using synthetic data and transfer learning to overcome these constraints and spread access to deep learning.

Finally, deep learning and neural networks are the most cutting-edge and consequential machine learning methods. Autonomous systems, natural language processing, picture and speech recognition, and automated learning have all been profoundly affected by their capacity to learn complicated representations from data autonomously. Despite deep learning's enormous promise, it comes with problems in interpretability, data needs, and computing resources. It will be essential to address these difficulties to ensure the appropriate and broad adoption of deep learning and ultimately harness its power to drive innovation and enhance lives across multiple areas.

Natural language processing (NLP)

Natural Language Processing (NLP) is a subfield of artificial intelligence (AI) and machine learning that focuses on the interaction between computers and human language. It encompasses a range of computational techniques for analyzing, understanding, and generating human language, enabling machines to process and respond to text and speech in meaningful and valuable ways. The applications of NLP are vast and varied, including chatbots, language translation, sentiment analysis, and more, making it an essential component of modern AI.

At the core of NLP is the challenge of understanding the complexities and nuances of human language. Language is inherently ambiguous, context-dependent, and full of idiomatic expressions, which makes it difficult for machines to interpret accurately. NLP addresses these challenges through various techniques and models that aim to replicate human-like understanding and generation of language.

One of the foundational tasks in NLP is text preprocessing, which involves cleaning and preparing raw text data for analysis. This step includes tokenization, where text is broken down into individual words or phrases; stop-word removal, where common words that do not carry significant meaning are eliminated; and stemming or lemmatization, where words are reduced to their root forms. These preprocessing steps are crucial for lowering language data's complexity and improving NLP model performance.

Word embeddings are another fundamental aspect of NLP. These are mathematical representations of words in a continuous vector space, capturing semantic relationships between them. Models like Word2Vec and GloVe (Global Vectors for Word Representation) have been instrumental in creating these embeddings. By mapping words to vectors based on their context within a large corpus of text, these models enable machines to understand word similarities and analogies. For example, in a well-trained word embedding model, the vector for "king" minus "man" plus "woman" should be close to the vector for "queen," illustrating the model's grasp of semantic relationships.

More sophisticated natural language processing methods, such as transformer-based models, have evolved from word embeddings. In 2017, Vaswani et al. introduced transformers, which completely changed natural language processing (NLP) by making it possible to analyze sequences in parallel and better capture long-range dependencies than earlier models such as RNNs and LSTM networks. Transformers can grasp context with greater nuance by employing self-attention mechanisms to determine the relative relevance of words in a phrase.

Introducing transformer models has led to developing powerful language models like BERT (Bidirectional Encoder Representations from Transformers) and GPT (Generative Pre-trained Transformer). BERT, developed by Google, leverages a bidirectional approach to understand the context of a word based on all surrounding words in a sentence, providing deep contextual understanding. GPT, developed by OpenAI, uses a unidirectional approach for generating coherent and contextually relevant text. These models have set new benchmarks in various NLP tasks, including question answering, text classification, and text generation.

Sentiment analysis is one of the most common applications of NLP. It involves determining a text's sentiment or emotional tone, such as identifying whether a product review is positive, negative, or neutral. Businesses use sentiment analysis to gauge customer opinions, monitor brand reputation, and make data-driven decisions. Companies can gain insights into consumer sentiment and respond appropriately by analyzing social media posts, reviews, and feedback.

Another significant application of NLP is machine translation, which automatically translates text or speech from one language to another. Early approaches to machine translation relied on rule-based and statistical methods, which had limitations regarding accuracy and fluency. The advent of neural machine translation (NMT), powered by deep learning and transformer models, has dramatically improved the quality of translations. NMT systems, like Google Translate, can handle idiomatic expressions, contextual nuances, and complex sentence structures more effectively than traditional methods.

NLP is also integral to developing chatbots and virtual assistants like Apple's Siri, Amazon's Alexa, and Google Assistant. These systems use NLP to understand user queries, retrieve relevant information, and generate appropriate responses. Chatbots and virtual assistants can perform various tasks by combining speech recognition, natural language understanding, and natural language generation, from setting reminders and providing weather updates to answering questions and controlling smart home devices.

Information retrieval and extraction is another crucial area where NLP plays a vital role. Search engines like Google use NLP techniques to understand user queries and retrieve the most relevant documents from the web. Information extraction involves identifying and extracting specific pieces of information from unstructured text, such as names, dates, and locations. This capability is essential for applications like knowledge graph construction, document summarization, and automated data entry.

Despite its advancements, NLP still faces several challenges. Ambiguity and context-dependency in language remain significant hurdles. For example, the word "bank" can refer to a financial institution or the side of a river, depending on the context. Handling such ambiguities requires sophisticated models capable of capturing context accurately. Furthermore, NLP models often need help understanding and generating language involving cultural or domain-specific knowledge, highlighting the need for continual improvements and domain-specific training.

Ethical considerations also play a crucial role in developing and deploying NLP systems. Issues such as bias in language models, data privacy, and the potential misuse of NLP technology for disinformation or harmful purposes must be addressed. Ensuring that NLP models are fair, transparent, and accountable is essential for their responsible and ethical use.

In conclusion, Natural Language Processing is a dynamic and rapidly evolving field that bridges the gap between human language and machine understanding. NLP has become an integral part of modern technology through techniques like text preprocessing, word embeddings, transformer models, and advanced applications such as sentiment analysis, machine translation, and chatbots. While challenges remain, ongoing research and advancements promise to enhance the capabilities and applications of NLP further, driving innovation and improving human-computer interactions across diverse domains.

Time series analysis

One subfield of statistics and data science, time series analysis, looks at patterns in sets of data captured at regular periods. This sort of analysis is essential for making educated decisions using temporal data, comprehending past trends, and predicting future values. Financial markets, economics, meteorology, ecology, and countless other disciplines rely on time series data.

The essence of time series analysis is examining data points gathered over a period of time to spot trends and patterns. Prediction accuracy relies on patterns such as seasonality, trends, and cyclical behaviors. The most common way to depict a time series is as a list of observations with a timestamp attached to each one. A key component of time series data analysis is the time dimension, which is unique among data types due to the data's inherent temporal ordering.

A primary goal of time series analysis is breaking down a time series into its parts—trend, seasonality, and noise. Whether the data shows an overall upward or downward trajectory is shown by the trend component, which reflects the long-term progression of the series. Data that exhibit regular, repeated patterns, typically driven by cyclical elements like seasons, months, or quarters, is said to be seasonal. Unpredictable fluctuations make up noise, also known as the irregular component.

Visualization is a typical tool for time series data analysis since it aids in identifying these components and comprehension of the series' behavior. Line plots are commonly employed to better understand the whole series across time and identify patterns like trends and seasonality. Furthermore, autocorrelation plots can reveal the interdependencies between the series across time by showing the degree of correlation between observations at different time lags.

One essential part of time series analysis is statistical modeling. Predicting future values using a linear combination of past values, the autoregressive (AR) model is one of the most popular and straightforward models. The order, which sets the number of lag observations in the model, defines the AR model. When predicting the next value, an AR(1) model looks at the most recent observation, whereas an AR(2) model looks at the two most recent observations.

The moving average (MA) model is another significant family of models. It produces future value predictions by averaging the mistakes in previous forecasts. The MA model also has an order, signifying the quantity of lags in the model's forecasts. Since it combines the autoregressive and moving average components, this model can capture both the effects of previous mistakes and the reliance on prior data.

The autoregressive integrated moving average (ARIMA) model is commonly used for non-stationary time series when the statistical features of the series change over time. Since the ARIMA model uses differencing to stabilize the series mean, it works well with trending series. Seasonal ARIMA (SARIMA) models are an extension of ARIMA that explicitly handles seasonal effects; they are necessary since seasonal patterns might further complicate the research.

Another complex method for time series analysis involves using the Kalman filter plus state-space models. In state-space models, the series is depicted as an equation system that describes the time-dependent evolution of the state variables. The Kalman filter is an algorithm that recursively guesses the state variables, making it a potent tool for filtering and smoothing time series data, especially in noise.

Time series analysis is another area where machine learning has made great strides. Sequential data is well-suited explicitly to methods like LSTM networks and recurrent neural networks (RNNs). Time series forecasting and anomaly detection are two applications that benefit from the topologies of these neural networks because of their ability to grasp intricate patterns and connections throughout time. With machine learning, these patterns may be learned directly from the raw data, giving the models greater flexibility and, in many cases, higher performance than traditional statistical models that frequently include manual feature engineering and assumptions about the data.

Forecasting is one of the primary uses of time series analysis. It entails making predictions about the series' future values using the data from the past. Precise prediction is essential in numerous fields. For example, predicting stock prices, interest rates, or market movements can help with risk management and investing strategies in the financial sector. In economics, policy decisions can be informed by forecasts of variables like GDP growth, inflation rates, and unemployment. Forecasting future demand is an integral part of SCM since it allows for more precise planning of production and inventory levels.

Anomaly detection relies on time series analysis to find out-of-the-ordinary patterns in the data. Anomalies, including manufacturing equipment breakdowns, financial transaction fraud, or unusual environmental circumstances, can signal significant occurrences or changes. It is possible to intervene quickly and reduce risks by detecting these irregularities in real time.

Time series analysis is also essential for reducing the impact of climate change and understanding its causes. To understand the effects of human actions on Earth, long-term climate data must be examined to detect patterns in weather variables like precipitation, temperature, and more. These findings can benefit environmental conservation and sustainability policies and strategies.

There are several obstacles to time series analysis, notwithstanding its many uses. Addressing missing data is a significant challenge since it can skew the analysis and cause erroneous predictions. In many cases, imputation techniques and rigorous modeling methodologies are the only way to fix this. Furthermore, conventional models struggle to account for the non-linear behaviors and intricate relationships that time series data often displays. More complex methods for evaluating and understanding time series data are becoming available due to developments in deep learning and machine learning, which are assisting in overcoming these obstacles.

In summary, time series analysis is an important and ever-changing area supporting numerous parts of contemporary science, economics, engineering, and finance. Analysts can unearth significant patterns, produce precise forecasts, and identify outliers through trend, seasonality, noise decomposition, data visualization, statistical model application, and machine learning approaches. Time series analysis is already crucial for generating innovations and informed decision-making across many disciplines, and its importance will only expand as the volume and complexity of temporal data grows.

Tools: TensorFlow, Keras, PyTorch

Researchers and practitioners in deep learning and machine learning rely on a handful of technologies that have become important. This group's three most popular and consequential frameworks are TensorFlow, Keras, and PyTorch. Artificial intelligence (AI) model developers can choose from various tools, each with advantages and disadvantages. To make the most of TensorFlow, Keras, and PyTorch in your machine-learning projects, you must be familiar with their features and how they work.

Google Brain's open-source TensorFlow library facilitates numerical computing and massive-scale ML. Thanks to its vast ecosystem, versatility, and robustness, TensorFlow has become an AI community cornerstone since its release in 2015. Machine learning models may be easily deployed across several platforms with TensorFlow, including computers, mobile devices, and edge devices. Due to its adaptability, projects requiring deployment in multiple environments are well-suited to TensorFlow.

TensorFlow's architecture aims to efficiently handle complex computations. It relies on data flow diagrams, in which nodes stand for operations and edges for the tensor data between them. This graph-based method shines when training massive neural networks since it allows for simultaneous processing and resource minimization. By providing high-level APIs like the Estimator API and Keras (now part of TensorFlow), TensorFlow makes programming more manageable and accessible for people of all skill levels.

The TensorBoard visualization toolset is a standout component of TensorFlow, facilitating model monitoring and debugging. Loss and accuracy metrics, computational graphs, and weight histograms are just a few ways TensorBoard illuminates model training. This visualization feature improves model performance and identifies problems. In addition, TensorFlow Extended (TFX) provides a full-stack solution for building production-ready ML pipelines, covering every step of the process from data import and validation to model serving and monitoring.

With an emphasis on ease of use and quick prototyping, Keras was created as a standalone API for high-level neural networks. Its easy use and straightforward design swiftly made it a favorite among programmers. With Keras's formal high-level API integration into TensorFlow in 2017, TensorFlow became even more user-friendly while still preserving its formidable capabilities. By hiding the ins and outs of tensor operations and backpropagation, Keras makes it possible to construct and train neural networks with minimal code.

Because of its modular design, Keras makes it easy to try out various neural network designs and components with little to no coding changes. You can build your models with ease because it works with many different types of layers, optimizers, and loss functions. You may quickly fine-tune the many pre-trained models included in Keras for specific applications. Some examples include VGG16, ResNet, and Inception. Models created on big datasets can be easily transferred to smaller ones with less training time and better performance because of this capability.

Even its extensive documentation and active community assistance are designed with the user in mind with Keras. Newbies can quickly become up and running with deep learning thanks to the comprehensive documentation and active community that offers a wealth of resources like tutorials, examples, and third-party libraries. By encouraging developers to work together and share resources, this ecosystem speeds up the creation of ground-breaking AI solutions.

Another prominent deep learning framework that has become increasingly popular since its 2016 release is PyTorch, which Facebook's AI Research group created. One notable feature of PyTorch is its dynamic computational graph, which enables users to make real-time modifications to the graph while running models. This feature makes PyTorch attractive to academics and developers who value quick prototyping and experimentation, as it offers greater flexibility and easier debugging than TensorFlow's static graph approach.

Since PyTorch is constantly evolving, it makes developing and debugging a breeze. Model behavior and intermediate outputs can be examined by developers using conventional Python debugging tools like PDB and print statements. PyTorch's transparency and ease of use have led to its popularity in academic research, where rapid iteration of models and ideas is crucial. The attractiveness of PyTorch is further increased by its simple syntax and smooth integration with the Python ecosystem. This integration enables it to be easily used with other scientific computing libraries, such as SciPy and NumPy.

PyTorch's support for sophisticated deep learning methods—including reinforcement learning, complicated neural network designs, and bespoke loss functions—is second to none. Backpropagation is made easier with its built-in automatic differentiation engine, Autograd, which allows for efficient optimization and computation of gradients. Natural language processing, computer vision, and generative models are just a few of the cutting-edge fields that have made PyTorch their go-to framework due to its expressiveness and adaptability.

With the release of TorchScript and the PyTorch JIT compiler, PyTorch has advanced dramatically in the realm of production deployment, complementing its research-oriented characteristics. To make it easier to deploy PyTorch models to production environments, developers can use TorchScript to convert them into an optimized subset of Python that is statically typed. Other tools in the PyTorch ecosystem include ONNX (Open Neural Network Exchange), which allows PyTorch to work with different frameworks. PyTorch Lightning is a high-level interface that makes training more accessible and code more readable.

Among the many powerful tools available for machine learning and deep learning, three stand out: TensorFlow, Keras, and PyTorch. TensorFlow's extensive ecosystem, scalability, and resilience make it an ideal choice for production settings and large-scale deployments. Thanks to its intuitive design and low learning curve, Keras is perfect for developers of all skill levels and is great for quick prototyping and experimentation. The research community favors PyTorch due to its intuitive coding and debugging processes, as well as its dynamic computational structure and flexibility. Combining these tools creates a robust and flexible toolbox that can advance AI and develop new solutions in other fields.

CHAPTER X

Data Science in Business

Use cases in marketing, finance, and operations

Machine learning and sophisticated data analytics have shifted paradigms in many sectors, including operations, marketing, and finance. These areas use complex algorithms and massive databases to improve operations, make better strategic decisions, and obtain insights. Thanks to the integration of these technologies, efficiency has been dramatically improved, and new opportunities for innovation and competitive advantage have been created.

Data analytics and machine learning have revolutionized marketing by allowing companies to better understand and interact with customers. Segmenting a large client base into smaller subsets defined by commonalities is one of the most common applications. Marketers may better segment clients by identifying trends in data from several sources, including purchase history, browsing behavior, and demographic information. Increased customer satisfaction and loyalty can be achieved through individualized marketing techniques suited to each segment's tastes and needs. One example is how e-commerce platforms enhance the shopping experience and drive sales using machine learning algorithms to recommend products based on individual browsing and purchase histories.

The marketing industry also extensively uses predictive analytics. Businesses can predict consumer and industry trends by looking at past data and seeing patterns. This expertise is invaluable when it comes to demand forecasting. With accurate estimates, organizations can better manage inventory levels, plan marketing campaigns, and allocate resources. To avoid overstocking or running out of stock, merchants employ predictive models to prepare for busy shopping times and adjust personnel and inventory accordingly.

Data analytics and machine learning are now vital in the financial sector when managing risks, detecting fraud, and developing investment strategies. By evaluating massive amounts of data, such as market movements, economic indicators, and past performance, financial institutions use these technologies to assess and reduce risk. Potential dangers can be identified, and early warnings can be provided by machine learning models, allowing proactive measures to be taken to avert losses. For instance, to decrease the probability of defaults, banks utilize predictive analytics to assess the creditworthiness of loan applicants by examining their work status, financial history, and other pertinent data.

Machine learning has also significantly influenced another crucial area: fraud detection. Identifying questionable activity in real time is possible by analyzing the massive volumes of data generated by financial transactions. Anomalies and patterns suggestive of fraudulent activity, such as out-of-the-ordinary transaction amounts or changes from customary spending habits, can be detected by machine learning algorithms. Financial institutions may now detect fraudulent transactions in real time, allowing them to prevent substantial damage. Credit card firms employ machine learning algorithms to track purchases and identify questionable ones to prevent financial harm to themselves and their clients.

Decisions made by financial analysts and portfolio managers in the investment world have been revolutionized by data analytics and machine learning. Quantitative models find investment opportunities and improve portfolios by analyzing large datasets, such as stock prices, trading volumes, and economic indices. A competitive advantage can be gained by using machine learning algorithms to discover patterns and correlations that would otherwise go unnoticed by standard analysis methods. For example, financial firms and hedge funds maximize returns while minimizing risks through algorithmic trading methods powered by machine learning. These strategies execute transactions based on complicated models.

Data analytics and machine learning have also been beneficial to operations management. Supply chain optimization is a well-known application. Businesses optimize their supply chains using machine learning algorithms that sift through data from many sources, including supplier performance, transit logistics, inventory levels, and more. Overall efficiency, delivery times, and costs are all improved by this optimization. Take manufacturing organizations as an example. They employ predictive maintenance models to monitor equipment performance and foresee when it might break down. This way, they can keep production running smoothly and minimize downtime.

Operations management also makes extensive use of demand forecasting. By minimizing waste and boosting service levels, businesses can benefit from accurate demand projections that help them align production schedules, inventory levels, and staff planning with anticipated demand. Machine learning algorithms forecast consumer demand by sifting through past sales data, current market tendencies, and exogenous variables like economic and seasonal influences. Industries like retail and manufacturing, which experience unpredictable demand patterns, greatly benefit from these capabilities. Businesses like car manufacturers utilize demand forecasting to organize their supply chains and production processes to avoid overproducing and still satisfy consumer demand.

Machine learning and data analytics are game-changers in transportation and logistics, especially when managing fleets and optimizing routes. Businesses use these technologies to analyze traffic patterns, weather, and delivery schedules to find the most efficient routes for their fleets. Through this optimization, fuel consumption is reduced, delivery times are minimized, and operational efficiency is enhanced. For instance, logistics firms can reduce operational expenses and increase delivery timeliness by using route optimization algorithms to plan truck routes.

In addition, data analytics and machine learning play a crucial role in industrial operations regarding quality control and process improvement. Machine learning algorithms can analyze production data for patterns and outliers that could signal quality problems. Companies may improve product quality and save waste by using this proactive approach and addressing issues before they escalate. Guarantee high-quality outputs while minimizing production costs, machine learning is used by semiconductor makers, for instance, to track the production process and identify faults early on.

Finally, marketing, finance, and operations have all benefited greatly from data analytics and machine learning. Optimal marketing strategies, predictive analytics, and targeted consumer involvement are all made possible by these technological advancements in the marketing realm. They improve financial decision-making, fraud detection, and risk management. With their help, operations may optimize their supply chains, demand forecasts, routes, and quality control. Data analytics and machine learning constantly improve, which bodes well for future innovations and efficiencies. It will help businesses succeed in challenging settings and reach their long-term goals.

Predictive analytics and customer insights

Businesses that want to gain a competitive edge by better understanding their clients and anticipating their demands now depend heavily on predictive analytics. By utilizing statistical algorithms, machine learning techniques, and historical data, predictive analytics helps businesses make well-informed decisions, optimize their strategies, and improve customer experiences. In today's data-driven environment, having the capacity to forecast future behaviors and trends based on historical and current data offers a tactical advantage.

The idea of utilizing past data to predict future results lies at the core of predictive analytics. Data must be gathered and analyzed from various sources, including transaction records, social media interactions, customer reviews, and browser activity. Businesses can find patterns and correlations in this data that would be impossible to find through manual means by utilizing sophisticated statistical models and machine learning techniques. These findings are then used to predict the tastes, trends, and behavior of future customers.

Customer segmentation is one of the most essential uses of predictive analytics. Businesses used to divide their clientele according to demographics like region, gender, and age. On the other hand, predictive analytics goes one step further by considering a wide range of factors, such as past purchases, internet activity, and social media usage. That makes it possible to create dynamic, highly detailed client groupings. To enhance the likelihood of sales, an e-commerce company may utilize predictive analytics to pinpoint a specific client segment that would react well to promotions on high-end products. It would allow for more focused marketing campaigns.

Personalization is another crucial area where predictive analytics brings tremendous benefits. By anticipating their preferences and behaviors, businesses can customize their services and interactions to customers' unique wants and wishes. This degree of customization improves client satisfaction and fosters a sense of loyalty. For example, streaming services like Netflix and Spotify use predictive analytics to suggest material based on past viewing or listening behavior. Higher retention rates result from these tailored recommendations, maintaining customer satisfaction and engagement.

Predictive analytics is essential for improving customer segmentation and customization and optimizing marketing strategies. By examining previous campaign outcomes and client feedback, companies can forecast which approaches will work in the future. That makes it possible to allocate marketing funds and resources more effectively. Retail companies can utilize predictive analytics to ascertain the ideal timing and content for email marketing campaigns. This approach guarantees that communications are promptly sent to appropriate customers to optimize engagement and conversion rates.

Many firms are concerned about customer attrition, and predictive analytics provides a potent way to deal with this problem. Businesses may prevent client attrition by seeing trends and telltale signs of impending churn. Predictive models can identify which consumers are most likely to leave by analyzing variables, including frequency of purchases, shifts in purchasing behavior, and customer feedback. Equipped with this data, companies can employ focused retention tactics, such as customized promotions or loyalty schemes, to re-engage high-risk clients and lower attrition rates.

Additionally, creativity and product creation are greatly aided by predictive analytics. Businesses can discover new requirements and preferences by examining usage data, market trends, and customer feedback. With this knowledge, businesses may better satisfy consumer wants by creating new items or enhancing current ones.

Predictive analytics, for instance, can be used by a computer company to examine how customers interact with a software product and pinpoint places where users struggle or regularly utilize specific features. The creation of new features or improvements that enhance the user experience overall can be guided by this information.

Predictive analytics is used in the financial sector to identify fraudulent activity and evaluate credit risk. Financial organizations use credit ratings, past transaction history, and other pertinent data to forecast a customer's risk of missing loan or credit card payments. It makes measuring risk more precisely and making wise financing selections possible. Predictive models can also spot odd trends or anomalies in transaction data, allowing them to spot potential fraud instantly. Predictive analytics, for example, is used by credit card firms to track transactions for indications of fraud, such as large, unexpected purchases or transactions in odd places, enabling early intervention to stop financial losses.

Predictive analytics also significantly impacts the healthcare sector, especially when it comes to bettering patient outcomes and operational effectiveness. Healthcare professionals can forecast a disease's course and identify patients at risk of developing specific illnesses by evaluating patient data, including medical history, treatment plans, and results. It enhances patient care and lowers healthcare expenses by enabling early intervention and customized treatment programs. Predictive analytics, for instance, can assist in identifying patients at risk of readmission following their release, allowing medical professionals to create follow-up care plans that lower the chance of readmission.

Predictive analytics has many benefits, but its application has drawbacks. Several essential aspects, including data availability and quality, can impact predictive model accuracy and dependability. Businesses must guarantee that they possess pertinent and high-quality data that has been appropriately cleansed and ready for examination. Furthermore, some companies may need help to acquire the particular knowledge and abilities required due to the complexity of predictive models. Realizing the full potential of predictive analytics also requires ensuring that the insights it produces are effectively conveyed and incorporated into decision-making processes.

Predictive analytics also has a crucial ethical component. Data security and privacy concerns arise when personal information is used for forecasting. Companies must overcome these obstacles by implementing robust data security safeguards and abiding by all applicable laws and moral standards. Sustaining trust and ethical norms requires openness in the application of predictive models and ensuring that consumers are aware of how their data is being used.

In conclusion, by enabling data-driven decision-making and offering profound customer insights, predictive analytics gives organizations in various industries a chance to undergo revolutionary change. Businesses may improve consumer engagement and loyalty by implementing enhanced segmentation, customization, and optimized marketing strategies. In addition, predictive analytics helps reduce customer attrition, directs product development, and improves risk management in industries like healthcare and finance. In today's data-driven world, the strategic application of predictive analytics can create substantial value and competitive advantage despite the difficulties related to data quality, complexity, and ethical issues.

Case studies of successful business applications

Successful corporate uses of machine learning and data analytics are increasing across various industries, proving these technologies' transformative impact on fostering efficiency, creativity, and competitive advantage. Several case studies demonstrate the practical applications of data-driven decision-making and the thoughtful incorporation of analytics into corporate procedures.

One noteworthy example is the retail behemoth Amazon, which has revolutionized its operations and customer experience by utilizing data analytics. Amazon's recommendation engine uses machine learning techniques to examine browsing and purchase patterns to provide tailored product recommendations. Sales and customer interaction have increased, greatly enhancing Amazon's performance. Predictive analytics is another tool that Amazon uses to streamline its supply chain management. It forecasts demand and inventory levels to guarantee on-time delivery and save expenses. Amazon has established a standard for data-driven decision-making and solidified its position as a leader in the e-commerce sector by utilizing data analytics.

American Express is one financial company that has effectively used data analytics to improve risk management and fraud detection. American Express utilizes advanced machine learning algorithms to instantly evaluate transaction data, detecting trends and deviations suggestive of fraudulent conduct. American Express has stopped millions of dollars' worth of fraudulent transactions yearly while causing the most minor inconvenience to its real clients because of this proactive approach. American Express also uses predictive analytics to evaluate credit risk and customize offers and rewards for each unique customer to increase client loyalty and retention. American Express has become a leader in the financial services sector and improved its competitive position by prioritizing data analytics and machine learning.

Another interesting case study is from the healthcare industry, where data analytics has improved operational effectiveness and patient care. Predictive analytics is used by the University of Pittsburgh Medical Center (UPMC) to lower medical expenses and enhance patient outcomes. UPMC can identify patients at risk of developing complications and forecast adverse events by evaluating data from medical imaging, electronic health records, and other patient information. This makes it possible for medical professionals to take preventative measures and offer individualized treatment programs. Furthermore, UPMC uses data analytics to streamline hospital operations, enhance resource allocation, and shorten patient wait times. UPMC has improved patient care quality and achieved cost savings and operational efficiencies by strategically utilizing data analytics.

UPS has used data analytics in the transportation and logistics Industry to streamline delivery processes and enhance customer support. UPS uses machine learning algorithms and intelligent analytics to optimize delivery routes while consuming less fuel and emitting fewer pollutants. UPS can dynamically modify delivery routes in real-time to minimize delays and maximize efficiency by assessing data from GPS trackers, weather forecasts, and traffic patterns. Moreover, UPS uses predictive analytics to forecast demand trends and package volumes, allowing for proactive resource allocation and capacity planning. By doing this, UPS can minimize expenses and adverse environmental effects while meeting customer expectations for prompt and dependable delivery. UPS has strengthened its position as a leader in the logistics sector by improving operational efficiency and customer happiness through its data-driven strategy.

Google has been a leader in the technology industry in continuously applying machine learning and data analytics to improve its products and services. Google's search engine uses advanced algorithms to swiftly provide relevant search results based on analysis of user queries. Google's search algorithms are continuously being improved by user feedback and behavior. It allows Google to deliver exact and customized search results, which enhances the user experience. Google also uses data analytics to target consumer ads based on their online behavior, interests, and demographics, optimizing its advertising platform. As a result, advertisers may maximize the return on their advertising investment while reaching their target demographic more successfully. Google has established itself as the top technological firm in the world by focusing unwaveringly on data analytics and machine learning. It has led to innovation and helped shape the digital landscape's future.

To sum up, these case studies demonstrate how data analytics and machine learning can revolutionize firms in various industries. Organizations across several sectors, including healthcare, transportation, and e-commerce, use data-driven decision-making to stimulate innovation, boost productivity, and elevate customer satisfaction. In today's increasingly data-driven world, firms can obtain essential insights, streamline operations, and gain a competitive edge by prioritizing data analytics and investing in cutting-edge technologies. Businesses looking to prosper in the digital age will continue to need to strategically integrate data analytics as the rate of technological innovation picks up speed.

CHAPTER XI

Data Science in Healthcare

Applications in medical diagnosis, treatment optimization, and patient care

Data science, a transformative force in the healthcare field, has revolutionized medical diagnosis, therapy optimization, and patient care. By harnessing the power of data science, healthcare practitioners can now deliver more accurate diagnoses, personalized treatment plans, and improved patient outcomes. This dynamic field leverages sophisticated analytical techniques, machine learning algorithms, and vast volumes of healthcare data, paving the way for a brighter future in healthcare.

Medical diagnosis is one of the primary uses of data science in the healthcare industry. Medical diagnosis has historically depended on the knowledge and judgment of medical practitioners, which can occasionally result in mistakes or discrepancies. A data-driven approach to diagnosis is provided by data science, in which algorithms examine patient information such as symptoms, medical history, test findings, and imaging data to produce precise diagnoses. By spotting patterns and correlations in the data that human clinicians might miss, machine learning algorithms can improve the efficiency and accuracy of diagnosis. For instance, based on patient data, machine-learning models have been constructed to diagnose diabetes, heart disease, and cancer, resulting in earlier detection and better treatment outcomes.

Treatment optimization is another critical area in which data science has significantly improved healthcare. Data science can assist healthcare providers in customizing treatment regimens to each patient's requirements and preferences by evaluating patient data and clinical outcomes. To determine the best interventions for each patient, this individualized approach to therapy optimization considers variables like lifestyle, medical history, and genetic composition. Machine learning algorithms can analyze large datasets to find trends and patterns in treatment responses, which can help create novel treatments and interventions. For instance, data science approaches have been applied to improve medicine dosages, forecast treatment results, and spot possible drug interactions. It has resulted in more efficient and individualized patient care.

Data science also alters patient care by enabling proactive and predictive healthcare interventions. Data science can identify patients at risk of problems or adverse events and take preemptive measures to reduce or mitigate these risks by evaluating patient data in real-time. For instance, predictive analytics algorithms can identify patients at risk of hospital readmission or declining health by analyzing electronic health records, vital signs, and other patient data. Then, to avoid negative consequences and enhance patient outcomes, healthcare practitioners apply focused interventions, such as medication adjustments, lifestyle modifications, or care coordination. Furthermore, data science can facilitate telemedicine and remote patient monitoring, which frees up healthcare systems by enabling patients to receive care and support from the comfort of their homes.

Data science, beyond its immediate applications in patient care, therapy optimization, and diagnostics, plays a pivotal role in healthcare research and innovation. By uncovering trends, patterns, and correlations in large-scale healthcare datasets, data science enhances our understanding of illness processes, treatment effectiveness, and healthcare outcomes. This enlightenment fuels creativity and research in fields like population health management, precision medicine, and medication development. Notably, data science enables the analysis of genomic data and the identification of genetic markers linked to disease risk, leading to the development of targeted treatments and individualized treatment plans. Moreover, data science empowers the analysis of real-world healthcare data to develop clinical practice standards, assess medical therapy efficacy, and enhance healthcare delivery, thereby fostering a culture of informed decision-making and innovation.

The extensive application of data science in healthcare confronts several obstacles despite its enormous promise. The complexity of healthcare data, interoperability problems, and privacy and security concerns are some of the main challenges to utilizing data science in healthcare to its fullest extent. Protecting patient data privacy and security is crucial, which calls for robust data governance frameworks, encryption standards, and access controls. Additionally, there are technological difficulties regarding data standardization, interoperability, and integration when merging data from many sources, such as wearable sensors, medical equipment, and electronic health records. Furthermore, processing, analyzing, and interpreting healthcare data successfully requires specialized skills and knowledge due to its frequent complexity, unstructured nature, and heterogeneity.

To sum up, data science has great potential to improve healthcare by facilitating more precise diagnosis, customized treatment regimens, proactive patient care, and creative research. Healthcare professionals can get essential insights from enormous volumes of healthcare data by utilizing advanced analytics techniques and machine learning algorithms. It can improve patient outcomes, enhance clinical decision-making, and improve healthcare delivery. The strategic application of data science in healthcare has the potential to transform illness prevention, diagnosis, and treatment, ultimately leading to improvements in the health and well-being of individuals and populations despite obstacles related to data privacy, interoperability, and complexity.

Case studies: disease prediction, personalized medicine

The transformative potential of data-driven approaches in healthcare is exemplified by case studies in disease prediction and customized medicine, which demonstrate how advanced analytics and machine learning algorithms can enhance patient outcomes and completely change the medical industry. Disease prediction models use many patient data, such as genetic information, medical history, lifestyle factors, and environmental exposures to determine who is most likely to get a given condition. These models can enable proactive treatments to prevent or lessen the onset of diseases by examining patterns and correlations within these datasets. That allows for the provision of early warnings.

In the area of cardiovascular disease prediction, there is one fascinating case study. To estimate a person's chance of suffering a cardiovascular event, such as a heart attack or stroke, researchers at the Framingham Heart Study developed a predictive model that examines several risk factors, including age, gender, blood pressure, cholesterol levels, smoking status, and family history of heart disease. The Framingham Risk Score is a model widely used in clinical practice to evaluate cardiovascular risk and direct preventative measures such as drug therapy, lifestyle changes, and routine monitoring. Healthcare practitioners can lower the frequency of cardiovascular events and enhance patient outcomes via the early identification of high-risk individuals and the implementation of focused interventions.

Applying machine learning algorithms to anticipate the onset of type 2 diabetes is another noteworthy case study in illness prediction. A predictive algorithm that evaluates laboratory test results, demographic data, and electronic health records (EHRs) has been developed by researchers at Stanford University to identify people who are at high risk of acquiring diabetes in the coming years. Using deep learning techniques, this model—dubbed the Deep Patient model—analyses vast datasets and discovers intricate patterns that point to early-stage diabetes. Healthcare professionals can postpone or stop the onset of diabetes by identifying people who are at risk and implementing preventive strategies, such as dietary and exercise interventions, lifestyle adjustments, and glucose monitoring. In the long run, this proactive approach to diabetes prevention can result in better health outcomes and lower healthcare costs.

Healthcare professionals can customize treatment plans and actions to each patient's particular needs, preferences, and traits thanks to data-driven approaches in personalized medicine. Personalized medicine seeks to maximize therapy efficacy, reduce side effects, and enhance patient adherence and satisfaction by evaluating genetic, clinical, and lifestyle data. Pharmacogenomics, which optimizes pharmaceutical therapy based on individual genetic profiles, is a well-known example of personalized medicine.

Implementing genotype-guided dosage for the anticoagulant warfarin is an interesting case study in pharmacogenomics. Due to the narrow therapeutic window of warfarin, it might be challenging to determine the ideal dose for each particular patient. Because genetic variations linked to warfarin metabolism and sensitivity have been found, genotype-guided dosing algorithms can now be developed to determine the best dose for each patient based on their genetic profile. Healthcare professionals can optimize treatment outcomes, lower the risk of side effects like bleeding or clotting, and enhance patient safety and satisfaction by customizing warfarin dosing based on individual genetic traits.

Targeted cancer therapy guided by genetic profiling is an additional example of customized medicine. Thanks to developments in genome sequencing technologies, scientists may find genetic mutations and variations linked to different kinds of cancer. By examining tumor genomes and contrasting them with standard tissue samples, oncologists can pinpoint therapeutically relevant mutations that propel tumor development and spread. With this information, tailored therapies that directly block the activity of mutations that cause cancer can be chosen, such as immunotherapies or medicines with molecular targets. Personalized medicine offers better treatment outcomes, decreased toxicity, and increased quality of life for cancer patients by customizing cancer treatment to the molecular profile of each patient's tumor.

To sum up, case studies in personalized medicine and disease prediction demonstrate how data-driven methods are revolutionizing the healthcare industry. These methods allow for early disease identification, preemptive treatments, and individualized treatment regimens that cater to each patient's specific needs and features by utilizing machine learning algorithms, advanced analytics, and large amounts of patient data. Healthcare professionals can use disease prediction models to identify patients at risk for a given condition and put preventive measures in place to enhance patient outcomes. Similarly, personalized medicine makes it possible to maximize the effectiveness of treatments, reduce side effects, and improve patient adherence and satisfaction. Data-driven methods have great potential to transform medical practice and advance precision healthcare globally as they develop and grow.

Ethical and privacy considerations in healthcare data science

Given the delicate nature of medical data and the possible consequences of its misuse, ethical and privacy concerns are critical to healthcare data science. Confidentiality and privacy of patients are among the main ethical issues. To maintain patient trust and comply with privacy laws like HIPAA (Health Insurance Portability and Accountability Act), healthcare data must be protected since it frequently contains highly personal information, such as genetic information, medical diagnoses, and treatment histories. To protect patient data from unwanted access, breaches, and misuse, healthcare companies and data scientists must put strong security measures, encryption techniques, and access controls in place.

Furthermore, openness and informed consent are fundamental ethical precepts in healthcare data science. Patients are entitled to information about how, by whom, and for what objectives their data will be used. Therefore, before gathering, retaining, or disclosing patient data for research or analytical purposes, healthcare professionals and researchers must have the express agreement of the patients. Patients are guaranteed to be aware of the advantages and disadvantages of taking part in data-driven research and to have the option to withdraw from the study at any time if they would prefer to keep their privacy unaltered.

Data bias and fairness are additional ethical factors in healthcare data research. Underrepresenting particular ethnicities or demographics in healthcare data might result in biased analysis and unfair consequences. To guarantee fairness and justice in their studies, data scientists must carefully assess the representativeness of their datasets and use strategies like data augmentation and bias mitigation. Furthermore, to allow healthcare professionals to comprehend the generation process and evaluate the accuracy and equity of the predictions, algorithms utilized in healthcare data science must be accessible and understandable.

Healthcare data science must address ethical issues, including data ownership and management. While people are the main parties interested in their health data, others, including healthcare professionals, researchers, and tech businesses, may also have access to and use this information. To guarantee that patient interests are safeguarded, and upheld, precise rules and laws are required to establish data ownership, rights, and duties. To control patient data collection, storage, and sharing while fostering data interoperability and collaboration for research and innovation, healthcare institutions must set up data governance frameworks and rules.

Lastly, applying machine learning and predictive analytics to the healthcare industry may provide ethical challenges. If predictive models are not adequately verified and calibrated, they may unintentionally maintain or worsen already-existing inequities and biases in healthcare delivery. Due to biases in the training data, algorithms used to predict treatment responses or patient outcomes, for instance, may unintentionally discriminate against specific populations or demographic groupings. By assessing model performance across a range of populations, keeping an eye out for biases and disparities, and putting fairness-aware algorithms and methodologies into practice to reduce unintended consequences, data scientists need to take proactive measures to solve these problems.

In summary, given the sensitive nature of medical data and the possible consequences of its misuse, ethical and privacy concerns are critical to the field of healthcare data science. Data scientists, legislators, and healthcare institutions must create precise policies, rules, and best practices to safeguard patient privacy, guarantee data security, and encourage the moral use of medical data. Healthcare data science can enhance patient outcomes, increase medical research, and spur innovation while protecting patient rights and fostering faith in the healthcare system by following ethical concepts, including transparency, informed consent, fairness, and accountability.

CHAPTER XII

Data Science in Social Media and Digital Marketing

Analyzing social media trends and sentiment analysis

For companies, marketers, and researchers looking to understand consumer behavior, public opinion, and new trends, sentiment analysis and social media trend analysis have become essential tools. Because social media platforms are so widely used and user-generated information is so abundant, social media data analysis presents many chances to comprehend and interact with consumers in real time. To help with strategy formulation and decision-making, analysts can assess sentiment, identify trends, and extract insightful information from social media conversations by utilizing advanced analytics techniques like machine learning and natural language processing (NLP).

Market research and customer insights are two leading social media trend analysis uses. Users of social media platforms freely express their thoughts, interests, and experiences in virtual focus groups. By monitoring social media interactions, businesses can obtain critical insights into consumer attitudes, product feedback, and new trends. For instance, companies can monitor social media mentions of their products or brands to determine customers' satisfaction, pinpoint areas for development, and immediately respond to their concerns. Social media listening technologies can also examine conversations centered around competitor names, industry keywords, or hashtags to spot new trends, market opportunities, and customer preferences. It helps companies stay ahead of the curve and modify their approach as necessary.

Opinion mining, or sentiment analysis, is another practical use of social media data analysis. Based on the language and context used, sentiment analysis algorithms categorize text data into positive, negative, or neutral sentiment categories. This helps companies determine how people feel about their campaigns, products, or brands and the general tone of social media discussions. For example, businesses can use sentiment analysis to gauge customer happiness, monitor sentiment shifts over time, and spot crises or reputational threats. Businesses may communicate with customers, proactively handle issues, and improve brand impression and loyalty by observing sentiment patterns.

Social media trend analysis may help with content production, marketing initiatives, brand message strategies, market research, and sentiment analysis. Businesses may seize chances to interact with their audience, generate traffic, and boost brand awareness by spotting hot topics, hashtags, and viral content. To find pertinent subjects and ideas to include in their content strategy, content producers should, for instance, keep an eye on the most popular hashtags on social media sites like Twitter and Instagram. Similarly, marketers can use social media data analysis to find brand advocates, influencers, and micro-influencers who can spread their message to new markets.

Social media trend analysis can also offer insightful information on how healthy marketing initiatives and advertising tactics work. Through monitoring key performance indicators (KPIs) like conversion rates, reach, and engagement metrics, companies can assess the effectiveness of their social media campaigns and adjust their marketing strategies appropriately. Marketers, for instance, can determine audience reaction to a particular campaign or product launch by analyzing the tone of social media discussions surrounding it. Based on this information, they can then modify their messaging or targeting. Furthermore, organizations may enhance and optimize their marketing efforts by using A/B testing and experimentation to determine the content, messaging, and ad formats that best appeal to their target demographic.

Sentiment and social media trend analysis have broader uses in public opinion research, social and political science, and crisis management than just business. Academics may analyze social media data to investigate popular opinion and sentiment trends about social issues, political candidates, or current events. This research might yield insightful findings. Similar to this, organizations and governments can monitor social media conversations to spot early indicators of disasters, public health emergencies, or civil unrest. That allows for prompt response plans and initiatives.

In summary, sentiment analysis and social media trend analysis provide insightful information about consumer behavior, industry trends, and public opinion. Utilizing social media listening technologies and sophisticated analytics methodologies, firms can obtain actionable information to guide strategy development, marketing campaigns, and decision-making. Today's business and research operations depend heavily on social media data analysis for anything from sentiment analysis and market research to content production and crisis management. For marketers, researchers, and organizations alike, the capacity to evaluate and comprehend social media trends will continue to be essential as social media continues to change and influence our digital environment.

Targeted advertising and recommendation systems

With the ability to reach specific audiences with individualized information and recommendations, targeted advertising and recommendation systems represent a paradigm leap in consumer engagement and marketing. These technologies use user behavior analysis, machine learning, and data analytics to provide customized experiences that speak to each user's needs, interests, and preferences. Businesses can optimize their marketing efforts, boost conversion rates, and improve customer happiness by utilizing personalized advertising and recommendation systems, which leverage massive amounts of data from several sources, such as browser history, purchase behavior, and demographic data.

The capacity of targeted advertising to present pertinent advertisements to the appropriate audience at the proper moment is one of its main benefits. Broad demographic or regional targeting is a common component of traditional mass advertising strategies, which can lead to low conversion rates and wasted ad expenditure. However, with targeted advertising, companies may divide their audience into groups according to demographics, interests, and other characteristics. Then, they show each group a customized set of ads that are more likely to connect. To increase conversion rates and drive higher returns on investment, an online retailer, for instance, can employ tailored advertising to suggest relevant products to visitors who have previously browsed comparable items or expressed interest in related categories.

That improves user experience and boosts engagement and retention; recommendation systems are essential for pointing consumers toward pertinent content, goods, and services. These systems provide individualized recommendations that suit the interests and preferences of each user by examining their behavior, preferences, and previous interactions. Recommendation systems can provide precise and pertinent recommendations by utilizing content-based filtering and collaborative filtering, allowing them to spot trends and similarities between people and products. Recommendation systems, for example, are used by streaming services like Netflix and Spotify to propose movies, TV series, or music based on a user's viewing or listening history, ratings, and preferences. It helps consumers find content that they are likely to love.

Additionally, companies may maximize the effectiveness of their campaigns and optimize their marketing strategies with the help of recommendations and targeted advertising systems. Businesses can obtain vital insights into what connects with their audience and modify their tactics by evaluating user data and measuring the efficacy of different ad creatives, messaging, and targeting methods. An e-commerce company, for instance, can use A/B testing to analyze the effectiveness of various call-to-actions, images, and headlines in their ads and then optimize their creative depending on the findings. Similarly, recommendation systems can monitor how users interact with suggested products or content and modify suggestions in real time to consider modifications in user behavior or preferences, making recommendations exciting and relevant.

Algorithmic bias, data security, and privacy are issues brought up by the growing usage of recommendations and targeted advertising. Arguments concerning consumer protection and privacy rights have been triggered by the gathering and use of personal data for targeted advertising. The fairness and transparency of recommendation systems have also been questioned about algorithmic prejudice and discrimination, particularly about jobs, housing, and financial services. To alleviate these worries, algorithms must balance providing individualized experiences and safeguarding user rights and privacy. They must also implement policies to reduce prejudice and guarantee equity and openness in decision-making.

To sum up, recommendation systems and targeted advertising give companies effective ways to connect with their target customers through tailored recommendations and content. Businesses may optimize their marketing efforts, boost conversion rates, and improve customer happiness by utilizing data analytics, machine learning, and user behavior analysis. Ethical and privacy issues must be addressed to guarantee that suggestion and targeted advertising are appropriately used and ethically, protecting user rights and privacy while providing tailored experiences that improve user experience and spur company expansion. Targeted advertising and recommendation systems will continue to be vital tools for companies looking to stay ahead of the curve and provide individualized experiences that connect with their audience as technology and consumer expectations change.

Case studies: social media campaigns, influencer marketing

The effectiveness of digital platforms and influencers in boosting brand visibility, engagement, and sales is demonstrated by case studies in social media campaigns and influencer marketing. Social media campaigns engage with audiences, magnify brand messaging, and accomplish marketing goals by utilizing the reach and virality of platforms like Facebook, Instagram, Twitter, and YouTube. Conversely, influencer marketing leverages the authority and popularity of bloggers, content producers, and social media stars to recommend goods, services, and companies to their audience. Businesses may tap into their devoted fan base and use influencers to attract new consumers and increase conversions by collaborating with influencers who share their values and target demographic.

A noteworthy example of a social media campaign is Wendy's, a fast-food business that has garnered significant recognition for its clever and captivating Twitter account. Wendy's is well known for its lighthearted and irreverent tweets, frequently joking about with both its fans and competitors' brands. In 2017, Wendy created the "Nuggs for Carter" campaign, which proved to be one of her most popular social media efforts. Carter Wilkerson, a Twitter user, initiated the campaign by inquiring about the number of retweets required by Wendy's to qualify for a year's worth of free chicken nuggets. In response, Wendy's issued a challenge: Carter would get his nuggets if he could garner 18 million retweets. The tweet went viral quickly, gaining support from corporations and celebrities and extensive media coverage. Despite not reaching the 18 million retweets target, Wendy's gave Carter a year's worth of free nuggets and donated to the Dave Thomas Foundation for Adoption. The ad demonstrated Wendy's capacity to use social media to interact with its audience, create buzz, and uphold its reputation as a lighthearted, personable, and customer-focused company.

Influencer marketing is an effective strategy for companies to engage their target market and increase revenue. The cosmetics company Glossier is one noteworthy example of a case study. Glossier has developed a devoted social media following through strategic alliances with influencers and user-generated content. Through its "Glossier Rep" program, Glossier enlists regular consumers, brand enthusiasts, and micro-influencers to help promote its products on social media. In exchange for telling their followers about Glossier events and sharing their experiences, these "Reps" get special discounts, early access to new products, and behind-the-scenes access. Glossier has developed a community-driven strategy for marketing that connects with its target demographic and encourages word-of-mouth referrals and conversions by enabling its customers to become brand ambassadors and advocates.

Another fascinating example of influencer marketing comes from the apparel company apparel Nova, which has established a billion-dollar business through strategic collaborations with social media influencers. Influencers from various channels, including YouTube, Instagram, and TikTok, work with Fashion Nova to present their apparel and accessories to their fans. These influencers provide sponsored content with Fashion Nova products, frequently styling or repurchasing the brands in their looks. Fashion Nova has successfully reached a wide range of stylish customers and increased in-store and online sales by capitalizing on the popularity and authority of influencers. The brand's success and quick growth in the competitive fashion business can be attributed to its influencer-driven marketing approach.

Influencer marketing and social media initiatives offer brands risks and obstacles even in the face of their triumphs. Customers are growing more skeptical of sponsored content and influencer endorsements that seem forced or unauthentic. Therefore, influencer marketers must maintain authenticity and credibility. Brands must thoroughly screen influencers to ensure they share their values, are relevant to their target market, and authentically engage with their followers. Furthermore, brands must be open and honest about sponsored content and paid collaborations to preserve credibility and adhere to advertising laws. To guarantee that social media initiatives connect with the target audience, accomplish marketing goals, and stay clear of controversy or backlash, rigorous strategy, implementation, and monitoring are also necessary.

To sum up, case studies in influencer marketing and social media campaigns demonstrate the success of using digital platforms and influencers to engage consumers, increase engagement, and accomplish marketing goals. Companies like Wendy's, Glossier, and Fashion Nova have shown how social media can spread brand messages, create buzz, and increase sales. However, social media campaigns and influencer marketing require strategic planning, authenticity, and openness to connect with customers and preserve trust. To properly harness the power of social media and influencers, organizations must modify their marketing strategies as social media continues to transform and shape the digital world.

CHAPTER XIII

Data Science in Government and Public Policy

Use cases in public health, urban planning, and policy making

Data science and analytics are being applied in fields beyond marketing and business, where they are vital in helping solve complex societal issues and guide public policy choices. Data-driven techniques provide creative ways to advance evidence-based decision-making, improve urban infrastructure, and promote community well-being in public health, urban planning, and policy making.

Data science is essential to epidemiological research, outbreak identification, and disease surveillance in public health. Public health organizations can track changes in population health, spot new health risks, and deploy resources efficiently by evaluating enormous volumes of health data, including medical claims, electronic health records, and demographic data. For instance, data analytics technologies have been crucial in the COVID-19 pandemic in tracking the virus's progress, identifying hotspots, and directing public health initiatives, including testing, contact tracing, and vaccination campaigns. Additionally, data science allows researchers to carry out extensive studies that determine risk factors, guide preventative measures, and assess the efficacy of public health interventions, which eventually improve health outcomes and lessen healthcare disparities.

Data-driven urban planning methods provide insightful information on environmental sustainability, transit patterns, and population dynamics. Urban planners might utilize geographic information systems (GIS) and data analytics to inform urban growth and infrastructure planning to assess variables, including population density, land use, traffic congestion, and air quality. For example, transportation authority's employ predictive analytics and traffic data to optimize traffic flow, minimize congestion, and increase the efficiency of public transit systems. Similarly, local governments can create sustainability programs and lessen the adverse environmental effects of urbanization by using statistics on energy use, waste production, and greenhouse gas emissions. Urban planning procedures can be improved by incorporating data-driven insights to build more resilient, livable, and sustainable communities that serve inhabitants' needs while protecting the environment and fostering economic development.

Data science gives decision-makers evidence-based insights to help them make decisions, assess the results of policies, and successfully address societal issues. Numerous social, economic, and environmental variables, including job rates, poverty levels, educational attainment, and crime rates, are the subject of massive data collection by government agencies. By applying statistical techniques, machine learning algorithms, and econometric models to analyze this data, policymakers can discern patterns, evaluate the consequences of policies, and formulate focused responses to resolve urgent concerns like social justice, poverty, and inequality. To encourage job growth and improve livelihoods, officials might use data analytics to identify neighborhoods with high poverty and unemployment rates. Then, they could introduce workforce development programs or offer financial incentives. Furthermore, data science empowers decision-makers to assess the success of current policies, pinpoint regions in need of development, and strategically distribute resources to optimize social welfare and accomplish policy goals.

Overall, data-driven techniques can alter complicated social situations and improve community well-being, as evidenced by the use cases of data science in public health, urban planning, and policy-making. Using data analytics, machine learning, and statistical modeling, stakeholders can obtain critical insights into population health trends, urban dynamics, and policy effects. It allows for well-informed decision-making and evidence-based interventions. And create healthier, more sustainable, and egalitarian communities, data science will play an increasingly important role in guiding public health efforts, urban development strategies, and policy decisions as technology develops and produces more data.

Case studies: predictive policing, public resource allocation

Two prominent examples of data-driven approaches in law enforcement and governance are predictive policing and public resource allocation. These approaches seek to maximize public safety, optimize resource allocation, and strengthen decision-making processes. Predictive policing uses machine learning algorithms to analyze demographic data, environmental conditions, and historical crime data to anticipate where and when crimes will likely occur. This allows law enforcement organizations to allocate resources and prevent crime proactively. In contrast, the allocation of public resources entails the utilization of data analytics to maximize the distribution of government resources, including cash, staff, and services, to effectively and efficiently address community needs.

The Los Angeles Police Department (LAPD), which used the PredPol predictive policing program to target crime hotspots and lower crime rates, is one impressive case study in predictive policing. To find patterns and trends in criminal activity, PredPol analyzes historical crime data using machine learning algorithms. PredPol creates daily crime forecasts that emphasize regions with the highest likelihood of crime by assessing variables like time, location, and crime. Using these forecasts, the LAPD may proactively assign police to certain areas, patrol those areas, and put preventative measures in place to stop criminal activity. Predictive policing improves public safety and prevents crime, as seen by the LAPD's claim of notable drops in crime rates in regions where it is used.

Governments can successfully meet community needs and goals by optimizing resource distribution through data-driven methods for public resource allocation. The city of New York, which launched the "Data-Driven Decision Making" (D3) program to enhance resource allocation and service delivery across numerous city agencies, provides one noteworthy case study. It identifies areas of need and allocates resources in a prioritized manner; the D3 program uses data analytics to examine various data sources, including 311 service requests, demographic data, and economic indicators. To proactively address issues like potholes, graffiti, and noise complaints, local agencies, for instance, utilize data analytics to identify neighborhoods with high rates of service calls. They then deploy resources, such as maintenance personnel or code enforcement officers, to solve these issues. Through the D3 program, the city has reduced response times, optimized service delivery, and raised residents' quality of life by utilizing data-driven insights.

Predictive policing and public resource allocation present ethical and privacy concerns about data usage, prejudice, and transparency, even with their potential benefits. Predictive policing algorithms, according to their detractors, may reinforce preexisting prejudices and unfairly target underprivileged communities, resulting in overpricing and discriminatory actions. Comparably, questions have been raised concerning the accountability and transparency of public resource allocation algorithms, especially about the selection criteria and their effects on marginalized communities. Ensuring that data-driven techniques are implemented ethically and equitably necessitates careful consideration of ethical standards, openness, and community engagement.

To sum up, case studies in public resource allocation and predictive policing show how data-driven methods can revolutionize public safety, optimize resource use, and strengthen governance. By utilizing machine learning algorithms and data analytics, law enforcement organizations and governments can obtain critical insights into crime trends, community needs, and resource priorities. That allows for well-informed decision-making and preemptive interventions. And guarantee the responsible, transparent, and equitable implementation of public resource allocation algorithms and predictive policing, it is imperative to tackle ethical and privacy problems. That will eventually foster public trust and confidence in data-driven governance endeavors.

Challenges and opportunities in government data analytics

Government data analytics offers both potential and challenges for strengthening public services, tackling social issues, and strengthening governance. Governments have access to enormous volumes of data, which can provide insightful information and opportunities for well-informed decision-making, but there are also substantial obstacles in the form of concerns about data privacy, organizational preparedness, and quality.

Ensuring the quality and integrity of data is a significant challenge in government data analytics. Government organizations gather and manage Large volumes of data from various sources, such as administrative records, surveys, and sensor networks. However, problems with data quality, such as errors, omissions, and inconsistencies, compromise the validity and dependability of studies and judgment calls. Ensure that data is accurate, dependable, and suitable for intended use. Investments in data governance frameworks, data management procedures, and data quality assurance systems are necessary to address data quality concerns.

In government data analytics, privacy considerations also present substantial obstacles, especially when handling sensitive or individually identifiable data. Concerns regarding data security, confidentiality, and privacy rights are raised because government organizations frequently process sensitive data about the public's financial, health, and demography. Protecting privacy and increasing public confidence in government data analytics projects require enforcing compliance with data protection laws, putting strong data security measures in place, and creating clear data access and usage policies.

Building capacity and ensuring organizational readiness are additional challenges in government data analytics. Many government organizations need more infrastructure, resources, and technological know-how to use data analytics efficiently. Furthermore, cooperation and knowledge exchange across departments and agencies may be hampered by organizational silos, bureaucratic procedures, and cultural obstacles. To overcome these obstacles, government organizations must invest in staff training, data literacy initiatives, and cross-functional cooperation to develop a data-driven culture that promotes innovation and learning.

Notwithstanding these obstacles, government data analytics presents several promising avenues for boosting public services, strengthening governance, and promoting evidence-based policymaking. Governments can obtain critical insights into population trends, service delivery outcomes, and policy consequences using data analytics tools and approaches. For instance, data analytics may assist governments in determining need areas, allocating resources wisely, and gauging the success of interventions in social services, healthcare, and education. Governments can also use data analytics to detect and reduce risks, predict future developments, and make well-informed decisions to improve citizen services and solve societal issues.

Furthermore, government data analytics can improve accountability, transparency, and citizen engagement by giving citizens access to information and insights that support decision-making and equipping them to hold their government accountable. Through public dashboards, data visualization tools, and open data programs, citizens can monitor government performance, access and analyze government data, and offer comments on policies and services. Government data analytics may boost democratic governance, build citizen trust, and encourage cooperation in tackling complex social issues by promoting openness and community involvement.

In summary, government data analytics has tremendous potential for boosting public services, strengthening governance, and promoting evidence-based decision-making, even though it poses issues with data quality, privacy, and organizational preparedness. Governments can overcome these obstacles and realize the full potential of data analytics to improve citizen services, address social issues, and create more responsive, transparent, and accountable government structures by funding data governance, data security, and capacity-building programs. Government agencies, commercial sector partners, and civil society organizations must work together to optimize the impact of data-driven programs and produce beneficial results for society as governments continue to leverage the potential of data analytics.

CHAPTER XIV

Emerging Trends in Data Science

AI and machine learning advancements

Technological developments in machine learning and artificial intelligence (AI) have changed several sectors by promoting efficiency, automation, and creativity in various fields. AI and machine learning technologies are changing how businesses function, how goods and services are delivered, and how choices are made across multiple industries, including healthcare, finance, manufacturing, and transportation. Thanks to the availability of large amounts of data, faster algorithm development, and higher computing power, AI systems can now execute complicated jobs, learn from mistakes, and adapt to changing settings.

Creating deep learning algorithms and neural networks is among the most important artificial intelligence and machine learning developments. In the machine learning branch of deep learning, multiple-layered artificial neural networks are trained to identify patterns and generate predictions from massive datasets. These neural networks have exhibited impressive capabilities in tasks such as image identification, natural language processing, and speech recognition, approaching human-level performance in some circumstances. For instance, deep learning algorithms underpin virtual assistants like Siri and Alexa, allowing them to identify speech, comprehend and react to natural language requests, and carry out web searches, reminder settings, and smart home device control. Furthermore, deep learning has transformed computer vision applications by allowing machines to process and interpret visual data—like surveillance footage, satellite photography, and medical images—with never-before-seen accuracy and speed.

The widespread use of reinforcement learning techniques is a noteworthy development in AI and machine learning. Through interactions with its surroundings and feedback in the form of incentives or penalties, an agent can learn to make decisions through machine learning called reinforcement learning. This method has been effectively used in fields where agents must learn complex behaviors and decision-making techniques, such as gaming, robotics, and autonomous cars. Reinforcement learning methods, for instance, have been used to teach robotic systems to accomplish superhuman performance in activities like gripping things, traversing environments, and even playing video games. Reinforcement learning also allows autonomous cars to learn how to maneuver through traffic, avoid obstacles, and make real-time snap decisions, opening the door to safer and more effective transportation systems.

Natural language processing (NLP) and language understanding have advanced due to AI and machine learning advances. Language translation, sentiment analysis, and text summarization are just a few of the applications made possible by NLP algorithms, which give machines the ability to comprehend, interpret, and produce human language. Language models, such as OpenAI's GPT (Generative Pre-trained Transformer) series, have proven to be exceptionally proficient in tasks like question answering, text production, and language translation; in fact, they have outperformed earlier state-of-the-art models in numerous benchmarks. These developments considerably impact applications where robots need to comprehend and produce natural language interactions with users, like chatbots for customer service, virtual assistants, and content creation.

Furthermore, new applications like personalized treatment, fraud detection, and predictive analytics are made possible by AI and machine learning developments, spurring innovation in healthcare, financial, and other industries. Artificial intelligence (AI) systems are utilized in the healthcare industry to evaluate medical pictures, identify illnesses, and forecast patient outcomes. It has improved patient outcomes, individualized treatment regimens, and diagnosis accuracy. Machine learning algorithms are used in finance to evaluate credit risk, identify fraudulent transactions, and optimize trading strategies. These tools help financial organizations reduce risk, increase operational efficiency, and improve compliance.

Even with these developments, ethical, equitable, and transparent issues still plague AI and machine learning. Concerns of prejudice, discrimination, and unforeseen consequences have been expressed as AI systems become more self-sufficient and capable of making decisions. Biased training data may cause AI systems to reinforce and magnify preexisting biases, producing unfair or discriminatory results. Additionally, it may be challenging to comprehend decision-making processes and hold AI systems responsible for their deeds due to some AI algorithms' opaque and unexplainable nature.

To sum up, AI and machine learning developments are bringing about revolutionary shifts in various sectors, fostering efficiency, automation, and creativity. Artificial intelligence (AI) technologies are transforming how businesses run, goods and services are given, and decisions are made. These technologies range from deep learning and reinforcement learning to natural language processing and healthcare applications. To ensure that AI helps society as a whole and reduces possible risks and downsides, however, ethics, fairness, and transparency issues must be addressed as AI systems grow more ubiquitous and autonomous. Collaboration and interdisciplinary methods will be essential to achieving the full potential of these technologies and ensuring their responsible and ethical deployment as academics and practitioners continue to push the boundaries of AI and machine learning.

Big data technologies: Hadoop, Spark

Organizations can now store, process, and analyze massive volumes of data in a new way, gaining valuable insights that help them make well-informed decisions. Big data technologies like Hadoop and Spark are part of this revolution. Massive datasets can be handled by clusters of commodity computers using Hadoop, an open-source distributed processing platform. The MapReduce programming style is used for parallel data processing, and the Hadoop Distributed File System (HDFS) is used for storage. Applications like data warehousing, log processing, and batch analytics are well-suited for Hadoop because of its distributed architecture, which enables businesses to store and handle petabytes of data with efficiency. Hadoop helps companies grow their data infrastructure affordably and handle big datasets in parallel, drastically cutting processing times and boosting performance. It is achieved by dividing data and computation among numerous nodes.

Contrarily, Spark is a quick and adaptable distributed computing framework specifically for processing large amounts of data in memory. In contrast to Hadoop's disk-based processing paradigm, Spark uses in-memory computing to process data interactively and iteratively up to 100 times quicker than conventional disk-based systems. Because Spark offers a single framework for machine learning, batch processing, real-time streaming, and graph processing, it's a flexible and effective big data analytics tool. Organizations can quickly develop end-to-end data pipelines and carry out complicated analytics activities thanks to Spark's expansive ecosystem of libraries and APIs, which includes Spark SQL, MLlib, and GraphX. Furthermore, Spark is a well-liked option for enterprises aiming to update their data architecture and realize the full potential of their data due to its smooth integration with Hadoop, cloud storage services, and other big data technologies.

For businesses to fully utilize big data and extract valuable insights from their data assets, Hadoop and Spark have both been instrumental. However, their approaches to data processing and their applicability for various task types diverge. The batch-oriented processing paradigm of Hadoop is ideal for applications that process vast batches of data without worrying about latency, like data warehousing, batch analytics, and ETL (extract, transform, load) procedures. However, low latency and high throughput are crucial criteria for real-time analytics, interactive querying, and iterative machine learning algorithms. They are well suited for Spark because of its in-memory processing capabilities. Combining Spark and Hadoop allows businesses to create dependable, scalable, and affordable big data platforms that satisfy their various data processing requirements while spurring innovation and expansion.

To sum up, Hadoop and Spark are two essential components of the extensive data ecosystem that let businesses economically store, handle, and evaluate massive amounts of data. Spark's in-memory computing capabilities allow for real-time analytics, interactive querying, and iterative machine learning, while Hadoop excels at batch-oriented processing and distributed storage. These complimentary technologies entities can construct adaptable, scalable, and multipurpose big data platforms that facilitate data-centric decision-making and open up fresh perspectives and prospects from their data reserves. Big data will only increase in amount, variety, and velocity. Hadoop and Spark will remain indispensable tools for businesses looking to turn their data into valuable insights and achieve a competitive advantage in today's data-driven marketplace.

The future of data visualization and storytelling

Data visualization and narrative have enormous potential to change communication and comprehension of complex information in the future. Effective data visualization strategies are becoming increasingly necessary as data volume, diversity, and velocity rise. Data visualization helps us to investigate patterns, trends, and relationships in data, making it easier to identify insights and communicate findings to varied audiences. But the future of data visualization entails more than just making static graphs and charts—it also involves utilizing cutting-edge approaches and newly developed technologies to produce immersive, interactive, and captivating storytelling powered by data.

The emergence of immersive and interactive visualization technologies, such as virtual reality (VR) and augmented reality (AR), is a significant theme influencing future data visualization. With the help of these technologies, users may engage and visualize data in three dimensions, making the experience more natural and engaging. For instance, users can examine data from various angles and better understand trends and patterns by using VR to view complex datasets in a virtual environment. Similarly, augmented reality (AR) allows users to engage with data in real time and contextually by superimposing data representations over the real world. These interactive and immersive visualization tools have the power to completely change the way we examine and comprehend data, opening up new avenues for interaction and narrative.

The use of storytelling techniques in data visualization to produce engaging tales is a significant trend for the future of the field. Using multimedia content, narrative devices, and data visualizations to tell a story and deliver important lessons is known as "data storytelling." By integrating data visualization with storytelling strategies like characters, plotlines, and narrative arcs, companies may craft compelling and unforgettable narratives based on data that effectively connect with viewers. Data journalism sources, for instance, employ narrative strategies to make data-driven tales come to life, enabling readers to relate to the data personally and comprehend its ramifications. Similarly, companies may utilize data storytelling to convey intricate information to clients, staff, and stakeholders, encouraging comprehension and action.

Furthermore, it is anticipated that developments in machine learning and artificial intelligence (AI) will significantly impact data visualization in the future. Organizations may produce data visualizations more effectively and efficiently using AI-powered technologies that automatically analyze data, spot trends, and deliver insights. AI algorithms, for instance, can assist users in creating visually appealing and educational charts and graphs by suggesting the best visualization types based on the features of the data and the target audience. AI may also evaluate how users interact with data visualizations to customize the representations and offer insights and recommendations that are specifically suited to them. These AI-driven tools for data visualization have the potential to democratize data analysis and visualization, opening it up to a broader audience and spurring creativity in the field of data-driven decision-making.

Furthermore, interdisciplinary approaches and increased collaboration will probably likely define the future of data visualization. Successful data visualization projects frequently involve collaboration between data scientists, designers, journalists, and domain specialists. Data visualization demands competence in design, statistics, and storytelling. Organizations may produce data visualizations that are enlightening, helpful, visually appealing, and captivating by combining a variety of viewpoints and skill sets. Multidisciplinary approaches can also encourage creativity and innovation in data visualization, which can create new methods, resources, and industry standards.

To sum up, there is a lot of promise for data visualization and storytelling in the future to change the way we communicate and comprehend complex information. Immersive and interactive visualization technologies, storytelling strategies, AI-powered tools, and interdisciplinary collaboration will shape the future of data visualization. These elements will allow organizations to craft engaging narratives based on data that compel viewers to understand and take action. Data will continue to play a significant role in innovation and decision-making. Therefore, companies that want to use data to drive change and accomplish their objectives must be able to visualize and convey data effectively.

CHAPTER XV

Ethics and Governance in Data Science

Ethical considerations in data collection and analysis

Ensuring that data-driven efforts respect people's rights, privacy, and dignity while producing insightful and practical results depends critically on ethical considerations in data collecting and analysis. Building trust with stakeholders and upholding social norms and expectations requires firms to emphasize ethical principles and values as they depend more and more on data to drive innovation, inform decision-making, and improve operations.

Getting the informed consent of the people whose data is being gathered is one of the most critical ethical factors in data collecting. By giving their informed consent, people make sure they are aware of their rights regarding the use of their data, how it will be used, and who will have access to it. This rule is especially crucial when private or sensitive data is being gathered, such as financial or medical information. Organizations must maintain transparency about their data-gathering procedures and furnish individuals with easily understandable information regarding the utilization and safeguarding of their data.

Ensuring data privacy and confidentiality is a further ethical factor to consider when collecting and analyzing data. Companies need to take action to safeguard people's privacy by putting strong data security measures in place, like encryption, access limits, and anonymization methods. Organizations should also reduce the risk of illegal access, disclosure, or misuse and only gather and keep the data required for the intended use. By prioritizing data privacy and confidentiality, organizations can reduce the risk of data breaches and privacy violations while fostering trust with stakeholders and individuals.

Organizations also need to consider the possibility of prejudice and discrimination in gathering and processing data. Throughout the data lifecycle, bias can appear in many phases, such as during data collection, preprocessing, and algorithmic decision-making. Biased studies and conclusions can arise from skewed or unrepresentative datasets, which biased sampling techniques or data-gathering tools can cause. Algorithmic bias can also occur when machine learning algorithms mirror the prejudices of their creators or learn from biased training data. Organizations must actively identify and reduce biases in their data-gathering and analysis processes to guarantee just and equitable results and prevent maintaining or escalating already-existing inequities.

Organizations using data-driven initiatives must also be mindful of possible harm and unforeseen outcomes. Organizations must foresee and reduce the risks and harms associated with data analytics and algorithms since they can substantially influence people's lives and communities. Automated decision-making systems, for instance, may unintentionally prejudice particular groups or exacerbate already-existing imbalances in sectors like lending, hiring, or criminal justice. Organizations must perform comprehensive risk assessments and ethical impact assessments to detect potential risks and damages. Then, they must put protections and accountability procedures in place to reduce the possibility of these risks and mitigate their effects.

In conclusion, ethical issues must be considered during the data gathering and analysis process to guarantee that data-driven projects respect people's rights, privacy, and dignity while producing insightful findings. Organizations can establish and maintain trust with stakeholders, reduce risks and damages, and adhere to ethical standards and societal norms by prioritizing informed consent, data protection, fairness, and responsibility. Organizations must incorporate ethical considerations into their data practices and processes, as data plays a central role in innovation and decision-making. It will ensure responsible and ethical data use and positive outcomes for individuals and society.

Data privacy laws and regulations: GDPR, CCPA

The protection of individuals' privacy rights, the regulation of the collection, use, and sharing of personal data, and the holding of organizations responsible for their data practices are all made possible by data privacy laws and regulations like the California Consumer Privacy Act (CCPA) in the United States and the General Data Protection Regulation (GDPR) in the European Union. These regulations seek to give people more control over personal information while encouraging accountability and transparency in data processing operations. They also reflect growing concerns about the privacy and security of personal data in the digital age.

The GDPR is one of the world's most extensive and far-reaching data privacy laws. It went into effect in May 2018. Regardless of the organization's location, it places stringent rules on entities that gather, handle, or keep the personal data of individuals within the EU. According to the General Data Protection Regulation (GDPR), organizations must obtain individuals' informed consent before collecting their data, only collect data for specific, explicit, and legitimate purposes, and only collect as much data as is necessary for the intended purpose. Other principles established by the GDPR include transparency, purpose limitation, and data minimization.

Furthermore, the GDPR gives people several rights, allowing them to manage how businesses use and share their data. These rights include accessing and correcting inaccurate personal data, the right to erasure (also known as the "right to be forgotten"), and data portability.

Comparably, the United States' historic CCPA privacy law was enacted in January 2020 to strengthen consumer privacy rights and raise data practices' accountability and transparency. Residents of California have rights under the CCPA to know what personal information is being collected about them, to request that businesses delete any personal information they may have on file, and to opt out of having their personal information sold. The CCPA applies to companies that satisfy specific criteria, such as generating more than $25 million in gross income annually or acquiring, receiving, or vending the personal information of at least 50,000 Californians, their residences, or their gadgets. In addition, the CCPA mandates that covered businesses obtain consumers' affirmative consent before selling their personal information, disclose their data collection and sharing practices clearly and conspicuously, and put reasonable security measures in place to guard against unauthorized access, disclosure, or misuse of that information.

Both the CCPA and the GDPR strongly emphasize accountability and adherence to data protection principles. To guarantee the ethical and legal processing of personal data, enterprises must put strong data governance structures, privacy policies, and security measures in place. Severe penalties can be imposed for breaking these rules: under the GDPR, fines can reach €20 million or 4% of the organization's yearly worldwide revenue, whichever is higher; under the CCPA, statutory damages can reach $7,500 per violation. These regulatory frameworks significantly impact businesses operating in California or the EU because they force them to invest in data protection measures, take a proactive approach to data privacy and compliance, and set up procedures for adequately handling data breaches and responding to requests from data subjects.

Data privacy rules and regulations like the CCPA and GDPR are crucial tools for safeguarding people's right to privacy, controlling the gathering and use of personal data, and encouraging responsibility and openness in data processing operations. These regulations allow people to govern their personal information and hold companies responsible for their data practices by clearly outlining the principles, rights, and obligations of organizations handling personal data. Since data is still essential to the digital economy, businesses must comply with data privacy rules and regulations to win customers' trust, reduce regulatory risks, and promote a privacy- and data-protective culture within their enterprises.

Building ethical frameworks and practices

To successfully traverse the complex ethical problems offered by data-driven decision-making, digital transformation, and technological developments, enterprises must develop ethical frameworks and procedures. Organizations may make ethical judgments, prioritize ethical concerns, and ensure their actions align with society's norms and expectations by using ethical frameworks, which offer guiding principles and values. By implementing ethical frameworks and practices, organizations can foster responsible and ethical behavior in their operations and relationships, reduce risks and damages, and increase stakeholder trust.

Establishing explicit ethical principles and values that represent the organization's commitment to moral behavior and responsible stewardship is crucial to developing ethical frameworks and practices. These principles may include values such as integrity, honesty, transparency, respect for human rights, and regard for the well-being of stakeholders. Organizations can foster a shared awareness of ethical expectations and obligations among employees, partners, and other stakeholders by clearly communicating these principles and incorporating them into the organization's culture, policies, and decision-making procedures.

Organizations must also create systems for locating, evaluating, and handling moral dangers and problems in their day-to-day operations. Foreseeing future ethical dilemmas and examining the possible effects of choices and actions on stakeholders and society may entail carrying out risk assessments, scenario planning exercises, and moral impact assessments. By proactively recognizing and resolving ethical risks, organizations can reduce the possibility of unethical errors, stop harm, and strengthen their ability to withstand ethical difficulties.

Organizations must also set up procedures and systems that encourage moral conduct and responsibility among all employees. That could entail giving staff members ethics education and training, setting up routes for reporting ethical issues or infractions, and putting in place systems for keeping an eye on and enforcing rules and regulations. Organizations can enable workers to act morally, voice concerns about immoral behavior, and hold others and themselves accountable for their deeds by cultivating a culture of ethics and accountability.

Additionally, to develop ethical frameworks and procedures, businesses must interact with stakeholders—such as partners, customers, employees, and communities—to learn about their expectations, beliefs, and concerns about moral behavior. Organizations can make sure that their ethical frameworks and practices reflect the larger societal context in which they operate and align with stakeholders' interests by requesting feedback, promoting discussion, and incorporating multiple perspectives into decision-making processes.

In conclusion, it is imperative for enterprises to consistently assess and modify their ethical frameworks and practices to adapt to evolving ethical, social, and technical contexts. It could entail reviewing ethical policies and procedures frequently, keeping an eye on newly identified ethical problems and trends, and modifying plans of action to take advantage of fresh chances and challenges. Organizations can maintain the relevance, efficacy, and alignment of their ethical frameworks and practices with changing ethical standards and public expectations by remaining knowledgeable, adaptable, and responsive.

To sum up, developing ethical frameworks and procedures is crucial for businesses to successfully negotiate the moral challenges posed by the digital era, cultivate stakeholder trust, and encourage moral behavior in all aspects of business dealings. Organizations can lay a strong foundation for ethical conduct and make sure that their actions align with societal values and expectations by fostering a culture of ethics and accountability, identifying and managing ethical risks, interacting with stakeholders, and regularly assessing and improving their methods. Organizations must be watchful and proactive in maintaining ethical standards and encouraging ethical behavior as technology advances and ethical challenges change to create a more ethical and sustainable future.

CONCLUSION

"A Guide to Data Science and Analytics: Navigating the Data Deluge: Tools, Techniques, and Applications" serves as an indispensable roadmap for navigating the vast and complex field of data science and analytics. With its comprehensive coverage of tools, techniques, and applications, the book equips readers with the knowledge and skills needed to harness the power of data for informed decision-making and innovation. From foundational concepts to advanced methodologies, the book offers valuable insights into the key principles and practices driving the data revolution.

Moreover, the book goes beyond technical aspects to explore ethical considerations, privacy regulations, and responsible data practices, ensuring that readers understand the broader societal implications of their work. By emphasizing the importance of ethical conduct and responsible data stewardship, the book empowers readers to use data science and analytics to create positive impact while minimizing risks and harms.

Whether you are a novice exploring the field or an experienced practitioner seeking to deepen your understanding, "A Guide to Data Science and Analytics" provides a comprehensive and accessible resource for navigating the complexities of the data-driven world. With its clear explanations, practical examples, and insightful discussions, the book inspires readers to unlock the full potential of data science and analytics to drive innovation, solve complex problems, and make a difference in today's data-driven society.

Thank you for buying and reading/ listening to our book. If you found this book useful/ helpful please take a few minutes and leave a review on the platform where you purchased our book. Your feedback matters greatly to us.